D1566835

Pleasures of the
TABLE

Pleasures of the
TABLE

A LITERARY ANTHOLOGY

selected by
Christina Hardyment

The British Library

CONTENTS

3 Love Bites   68

4 Childish Things   96

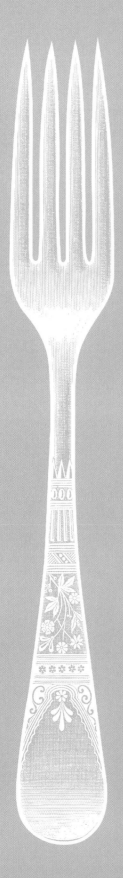

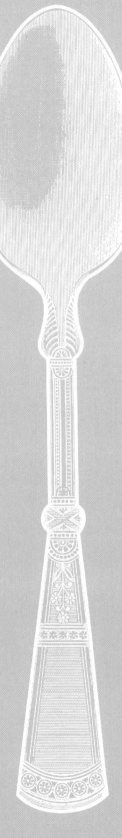

8   Literary Recipes   200

INTRODUCTION

If more of us valued food and cheer and song above hoarded gold, it would be a merrier world. (JRR Tolkien, *The Hobbit*, 1937)

What does cookery mean? It means the knowledge of Medea, and of Circe, and of Calypso, and of Helen, and of Rebekah, and of the Queen of Sheba. It means knowledge of all herbs, and fruits, and balms, and spices, and of all that is healing and sweet in groves, and savoury in meat. It means carefulness and inventiveness, watchfulness, willingness, and readiness of appliances. It means the economy of your great-grandmother, and the science of modern chemistry, and French art, and Arabian hospitality. It means, in fine, that you are to see imperatively that every one has something nice to eat. (John Ruskin, *Ethics of the Dust*,1865)

Napoleon famously declared that an army marched on its stomach; less familiar is the idea that great authors were as eager to feed their stomachs as their imaginations. Passages describing food abound in novels – perhaps most famous is Marcel Proust's episode of the madeleine – and meals often play an important part in a story: the White Witch's Turkish Delight; Sherlock Holmes' breakfast surprise. Poets apostrophise the delights of eating both in the grand style and modestly, and use food to tempt and seduce. Alexandre Dumas wrote the authoritative *Le Grand dictionnaire de cuisine* as well as novels galore, and cooks such as Robert May, Alexis Soyer and Elizabeth David are so enjoyable to read that I have decided they have a place in literature as well as in the kitchen.

The anthology begins with the important matter of making your guests – and your own loved ones – feel comfortable as they eat. Surroundings can be as important as the food served, argues the Georgian essayist Thomas Walker as he describes the ideal dining room;

for George Gissing the ceremony of afternoon tea shows English hospitality in its 'kindliest aspect', and in *To the Lighthouse* Virginia Woolf's Mrs Ramsay makes a splendid *boeuf en daube* the celebratory centre of a family meal.

Next comes eating to impress. I couldn't resist Robert May's revelation of just how those famous pies filled with real birds (and in his case frogs) were created, or Miguel de Cervantes' account of Sancho Panza goggling at Camacho's lavish wedding feast with its vast cauldrons of game and its fifty cook-maids, 'clean, brisk and blithe'. Washington Irving salivates over the 'whole family of cakes' and bowls of cream at a Dutch feast in Sleepy Hollow, and Gustave Flaubert makes aphrodisiac scents at an aristocratic dinner party the prelude to the downfall of Madame Bovary.

Honoré de Balzac warned that 'great love affairs start with champagne and end with tisane', and there is no doubt that in literature food and love go together rather better than love and marriage. Mrs Waters seduces Tom Jones over dinner; John Keats, Lord Byron and DH Lawrence fill up the senses with erotic accounts of spiced dainties, pomegranate sherbets and the 'delicious rottenness' of medlars.

Many of our most vivid memories of food in literature were laid down in childhood, be it Pinocchio aching with hunger, Heidi enjoying toasted cheese and milk straight from the cow in her grandfather's alpine hut, or 'robber tea' in John Masefield's *The Box of Delights*. Food also has its perils: Christina Rossetti uses forbidden fruits as an instrument of seduction in 'Goblin Market', and in *The Lion, the Witch and the Wardrobe*, the White Witch's enchanted Turkish Delight makes Edmund forget all loyalty to his brother and sisters. Of course, cooking while camping on an island is every child's favourite dream, be it scrambling eggs on Arthur Ransome's Wild Cat Island, or picnicking on Enid Blyton's Kirrin Island where food 'always tastes better out of doors'.

My section on Distant Times and Places offers Petronius' account of Trimalchio's excesses, seethed tortoise in ancient China and seal's liver fried in penguin blubber as a treat for Captain Scott. There is a mathematically designed feast for Gulliver in Laputa, and generous give-and-take in Africa between David Livingstone and Sekeletu, chief of the Makalolo. Finally, Herman Melville waxes lyrical on the clam and cod chowders that Ishmael and Queequeg gobble up at the Try Pots Inn in Nantucket.

Much as I've enjoyed exploring accounts of gourmet excesses, my own tastes tend towards simple things: Sydney Smith's subtle salad dressing, William Thackeray's 'smoking and tender and juicy' mutton, Jerome K Jerome's supper on the river, and probably excessive descriptions of honey, tea and toast by authors as varied as Sir Kenelm Digby, William Cowper and Kenneth Grahame.

Finally, I've gathered a couple of dozen recipes, either taken from literature or beloved by authors, so that you can try them for yourself: Izaak Walton's method of cooking trout, Alexis Soyer's Balaklava Nectar and Emily Dickinson's gingerbread. I haven't myself tried Hannah Glasse's method of raising a salad in two hours on fresh horse-dung, but I can thoroughly recommend Omelette Arnold Bennett (still served in London's Savoy Grill) and George Orwell's method of brewing tea. My exploration of literary eating will I hope amuse and surprise you, make your mouth water and encourage culinary experiment.

1 The Art of Hospitality

*We should look for someone to eat and
drink with before looking for something
to eat and drink.*

Epicurus

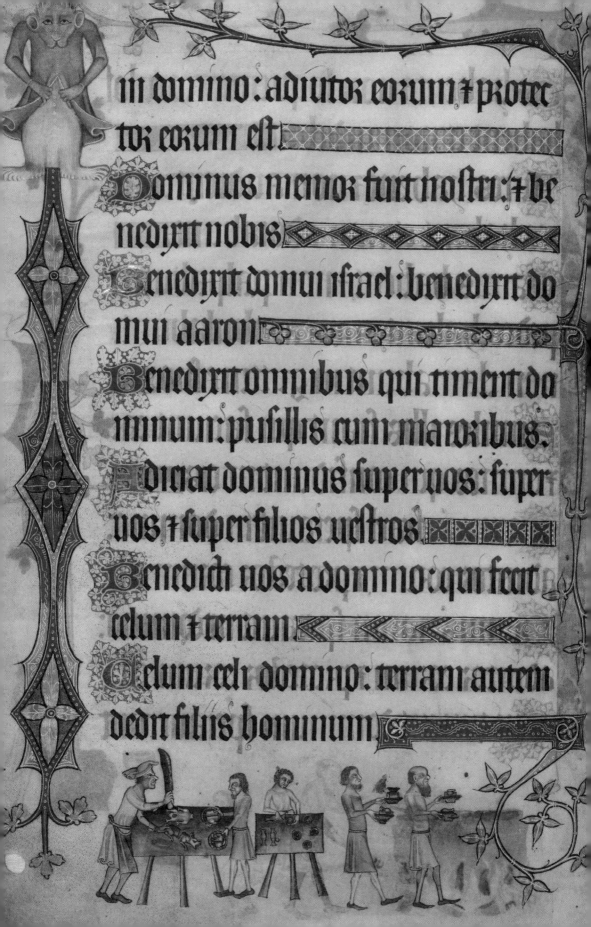

in domino : adiutor eorum + protec
tor eorum est.

Dominus memor fuit nostri : + be
nedixit nobis.

Benedixit domui israel : benedixit do
mui aaron.

Benedixit omnibus qui timent do
minum : pusillis cum maioribus.

Adiciat dominus super uos : super
uos + super filios uestros.

Benedicti uos a domino : qui fecit
celum + terram.

Celum celi domino : terram autem
dedit filiis hominum.

✕ Epicurus' Very Son

Geoffrey Chaucer (1343–1400) evidently approved of the whole-hearted welcome received by guests who were invited to his Franklin's house (Prologue, Canterbury Tales, *translated by Neville Coghill).*

There was a Franklin with him, it appeared;
White as a daisy-petal was his beard.
A sanguine man, high-coloured and benign,
He loved a morning sop of cake in wine.
He lived for pleasure and had always done,
For he was Epicurus' very son,
In whose opinion sensual delight
Was the one true felicity in sight.
As noted as St. Julian was for bounty
He made his household free to all the County.
His bread, his ale were finest of the fine
And no one had a better stock of wine.
His house was never short of bake-meat pies,
Of fish and flesh, and these in such supplies
It positively snowed with meat and drink
And all the dainties that a man could think.
According to the seasons of the year
Changes of dish were ordered to appear.
He kept fat partridges in coops, beyond,
Many a bream and pike were in his pond.
Woe to the cook unless the sauce was hot
And sharp, or if he wasn't on the spot!
And in his hall a table stood arrayed
And ready all day long, with places laid.
As Justice at the Sessions none stood higher;
He often had been Member for the Shire.
A dagger and a little purse of silk
Hung at his girdle, white as morning milk.
As Sheriff he checked audit, every entry.
He was a model among landed gentry.

Good Cheer

A chorister of St Paul's Cathedral and Eton, and educated at King's College, Cambridge, Thomas Tusser (1524–1580) had a fine ear for a rhyme. He spent ten years at court as a musician before marrying and settling down to farm in Sussex. Five Hundred Points of Good Husbandry (1573), his famous advice book for farming families, is full of insights into daily life in Tudor times.

Good husband and housewife, now chiefly be glad,
Things handsome to have, as they ought to be had.
They both do provide, against Christmas do come,
To welcome their neighbours, good cheer to have some.
Good bread and good drink, a good fire in the hall,
Brawn, pudding, and souse, and good mustard withal.
Beef, mutton, and pork, and good pies of the best,
Pig, veal, goose, and capon, and turkey well drest,
Cheese, apples and nuts, and good carols to hear,
As then in the country is counted good cheer.
What cost to good husband, is any of this?
Good household provision only it is:
Of other the like, I do leave out a many,
That costeth the husband never a penny.

Inviting a Friend to Supper

The satirical poet and dramatist Ben Jonson (1572–1637) published this charming description of a homely feast in 1616. A decade earlier he had been out of favour at court because of his attendance in 1605 at a dinner eaten by the Gunpowder Plotters, which puts an interesting slant on the seven last lines. Knats [more commonly knots], rails and ruffs (l.20) are all small birds.

Tonight, grave sir, both my poor house, and I
Do equally desire your company;
Not that we think us worthy such a guest,
But that your worth will dignify our feast
With those that come, whose grace may make that seem
Something, which else could hope for no esteem.
It is the fair acceptance, sir, creates
The entertainment perfect, not the cates [delicacies].
Yet shall you have, to rectify your palate,
An olive, capers, or some better salad
Ushering the mutton; with a short-legged hen,
If we can get her, full of eggs, and then
Lemons, and wine for sauce; to these a coney [rabbit]
Is not to be despaired of, for our money;
And, though fowl now be scarce, yet there are clerks,
The sky not falling, think we may have larks.
I'll tell you of more, and lie, so you will come:
Of partridge, pheasant, woodcock, of which some
May yet be there, and godwit, if we can;
Knat, rail, and ruff too. Howsoe'er, my man
Shall read a piece of Virgil, Tacitus,
Livy, or of some better book to us,
Of which we'll speak our minds, amidst our meat;
And I'll profess no verses to repeat.
To this, if ought appear which I not know of,
That will the pastry, not my paper, show of.
Digestive cheese and fruit there sure will be;
But that which most doth take my Muse and me,

Is a pure cup of rich Canary wine,
Which is the Mermaid's now, but shall be mine;
Of which had Horace, or Anacreon tasted,
Their lives, as so their lines, till now had lasted.
Tobacco, nectar, or the Thespian spring,
Are all but Luther's beer to this I sing.
Of this we will sup free, but moderately,
And we will have no Pooley, or Parrot by,
Nor shall our cups make any guilty men;
But, at our parting we will be as when
We innocently met. No simple word
That shall be uttered at our mirthful board,
Shall make us sad next morning or affright
The liberty that we'll enjoy tonight.

✕ I Find My New Table Very Proper

Samuel Pepys (1633–1703) describes his first dinner party in his new house with both anxiety and complacency. Dr Clerke and Mr Pierce had been with him on the expedition to bring Charles II back to England.

13 January 1663

So my poor wife rose by five o'clock in the morning, before day, and went to market and bought fowls and many other things for dinner, with which I was highly pleased, and the chine of beef was down also before six o'clock, and my own jack, of which I was doubtful, do carry it very well.

Things being put in order, and the cook come, I went to the office, where we sat till noon and then broke up, and I home, whither by and by comes Dr Clerke and his lady, his sister, and a she-cousin, and Mr Pierce and his wife, which was all my guests. I had for them, after oysters, at first course, a hash of rabbits, a lamb, and a rare chine of beef. Next a great dish of roasted fowl, cost me about 30s., and a tart, and then fruit and cheese. My dinner was noble and enough. I had my house mighty clean and neat; my room below with a good fire in it; my dining-room above, and my chamber being made a withdrawing-chamber; and my wife's a good fire also. I find my new table very proper, and will hold nine or ten people well, but eight with great room. After dinner the women to cards in my wife's chamber, and the Dr and Mr Pierce in mine, because the dining-room smokes unless I keep a good charcoal fire, which I was not then provided with. At night to supper, had a good sack posset and cold meat, and sent my guests away about ten o'clock at night, both them and myself highly pleased with our management of this day; and indeed their company was very fine, and Mrs Clerke a very witty, fine lady, though a little conceited and proud. So weary, so to bed. I believe this day's feast will cost me near £5.

✗ Bountiful Breakfasts

Sir Walter Scott (1771–1832) only ate twice a day – a 'bountiful' breakfast and a 'very moderate' dinner. Bountiful breakfasts recur in his novels: here are a trio of them – two Scottish and one French.

John Graham of Claverhouse Breakfasts at Tillietudlem
(*Old Mortality*, 1816)

The breakfast of Lady Margaret Bellenden no more resembled a modern déjeuner, than the great stone hall at Tillietudlem could brook comparison with a modern drawing-room. No tea, no coffee, no variety of rolls, but solid and substantial viands – the priestly ham, the knightly sirloin, the noble baron of beef, the princely venison pasty; while silver flagons, saved with difficulty from the claws of Covenanters, now mantled, some with ale, some with mead, and some with generous wine of various qualities and descriptions. The appetites of the guests were in correspondence to the magnificence and solidity of the preparation – no piddling – no boy's-play, but that steady and persevering exercise of the jaws which is best learned by early morning hours, and by occasional hard commons.

Lady Margaret beheld with delight the cates which she had provided descending with such alacrity into the persons of her honoured guests, and had little occasion to exercise, with respect to any of the company saving Claverhouse himself, the compulsory urgency of pressing to eat, to which, as to the *peine forte et dure*, the ladies of that period were in the custom of subjecting their guests.

Edward Waverley Breakfasts with the Rose of Tully-Veolan
(*Waverley*, 1814)

He descended to the breakfast parlour with the intention of taking leave of the family, and writing to one of his brother officers to meet him at the inn midway between Tully-Veolan and the town where they were quartered, in order that he might convey such a message to the Laird of Balmawhapple as the circumstances seemed to demand.

He found Miss Bradwardine presiding over the tea and coffee, the table loaded with warm bread, both of flour, oatmeal, and barley meal, in the shape of loaves, cakes, biscuits, and other varieties, together with eggs, reindeer ham, mutton and beef ditto, smoked salmon, marmalade, and all the other delicacies which induced even Johnson himself to extol the luxury of a Scotch breakfast above that of all other countries. A mess of oatmeal porridge, flanked by a silver jug, which held an equal mixture of cream and butter-milk, was placed for the Baron's share of this repast.

Quentin Durward Breakfasts With an Incognito King at Tours (*Quentin Durward,* 1823)

The breakfast was … admirable. There was a pâté de Perigord over which a gastronome would have wished to live and die, like Homer's lotus-eaters, forgetful of kin, native country, and all social obligations whatsoever. Its vast walls of magnificent crust seemed raised like the bulwarks of some rich metropolitan city, an emblem of the wealth with they are designed to protect. There was a delicate ragout, with just that petit point de l'ail [hint of garlic] which Gascons love, and Scottishmen do not hate.

There was, besides, a delicate ham which had once supported a noble wild boar in the neighbouring wood of Mountrichart. There was the most exquisite white bread, made into little round loaves called boules (whence the bakers took their French name of boulangers) of which the crust was so inviting that, even with water alone, it would have been a delicacy. He threw himself upon the ragout and the plate was presently vacant. He attacked the mighty pastry, marched deep into the bowels of the land and, seasoning his enormous meal with an occasional cup of wine, returned to the charge again and again.

✗ One of Our Small Eggs Will Not Hurt You

Jane Austen (1775–1817) delighted in veiled irony, perfectly executed in her account of supper after the evening card party given at Hartfield by Emma and her valetudinarian father, and Emma's consequent decision to take the orphaned Harriet Smith under her wing (Emma, 1815).

The evening flew away at a very unusual rate; and the supper-table, which always closed such parties, and for which [Emma] had been used to sit and watch the due time, was all set out and ready, and moved forwards to the fire, before she was aware. With an alacrity beyond the common impulse of a spirit which yet was never indifferent to the credit of doing every thing well and attentively, with the real good-will of a mind delighted with its own ideas, did she then do all the honours of the meal, and help and recommend the minced chicken and scalloped oysters, with an urgency which she knew would be acceptable to the early hours and civil scruples of their guests.

Upon such occasions poor Mr Woodhouse's feelings were in sad warfare. He loved to have the cloth laid, because it had been the fashion of his youth, but his conviction of suppers being very unwholesome made him rather sorry to see any thing put on it; and while his hospitality would have welcomed his visitors to every thing, his care for their health made him grieve that they would eat.

Such another small basin of thin gruel as his own was all that he could, with thorough self-approbation, recommend; though he might constrain himself, while the ladies were comfortably clearing the nicer things, to say:

'Mrs Bates, let me propose your venturing on one of these eggs. An egg boiled very soft is not unwholesome. Serle understands boiling an egg better than any body. I would not recommend an egg boiled by any body else; but you need not be afraid, they are very small, you see – one of our small eggs will not hurt you. Miss Bates, let Emma help you to a little bit of tart – a very little bit. Ours are all apple-tarts. You need not be afraid of unwholesome preserves here. I do not advise the custard. Mrs Goddard, what say you to half a glass of wine? A small

half-glass, put into a tumbler of water? I do not think it could disagree with you.'

Emma allowed her father to talk — but supplied her visitors in a much more satisfactory style, and on the present evening had particular pleasure in sending them away happy. The happiness of Miss Smith was quite equal to her intentions. Miss Woodhouse was so great a personage in Highbury, that the prospect of the introduction had given as much panic as pleasure; but the humble, grateful little girl went off with highly gratified feelings, delighted with the affability with which Miss Woodhouse had treated her all the evening, and actually shaken hands with her at last!

✂ The Ideal Dining Room

Thomas Walker (1784–1836), a Lambeth police magistrate and author of Aristology, or The Art of Dining *(1835) was the son of a Manchester manufacturer, and imbued with the Methodist love of simplicity.*

Spacious and lofty rooms destroy, or at least weaken, that feeling of concentration which is essential to perfect fellowship. There is a sort of evaporation of one's self, or flying off into the void, which impairs that force of attention necessary to give and receive complete enjoyment. A party, to use a familiar phrase, should be, as it were, boxed up, comfortably packed, with room enough, but not to spare, or, as the French revolutionists used to have it, should be 'one and indivisible'. Those who have dined in the very small rooms, called *cabinets particuliers* at the restaurants at Paris, must have remarked the beneficial influence of compactness in promoting hilarity, and banishing abstraction and restraint; but those rooms have no other desirable qualification but their smallness, which is often extreme, and they have not been originally contrived for the purpose for which they are used, yet they have a capability of producing more of a festive disposition than is to be found amidst space and display.

Dining-rooms in London are in general, I think, very tasteless and uninspiring in themselves, and, when set out, they are decorated, after the barbarian style, rather for display, than with reference to their use. From the architect to the table-decorator, there seems to be a total absence of genius for the real objects to be aimed at. Justness of proportion, harmony of colouring, and disposition of light, are the most desirable qualities in any room, but especially in a dining-room, without any individual ornaments or objects to distract the attention; so that the moment one enters, there may be a feeling of fitness, which is productive of undisturbed satisfaction, and disposes the mind to the best state for enjoyment. Attention should be directed to produce an effect from the whole, and not by the parts.

For this reason light should be thrown in the least observable manner, and not ostentatiously from ornamental objects. There should be the pleasing effect of good light, with the least perception whence

it comes. There is no art in lighting a table by cumbrous branches; but there is in throwing a light upon it, like some of Rembrandt's paintings, and the effect is accordingly. The first is vulgar; the latter refined. In the same manner light from windows should be admitted only with reference to the table; and during dinner the view should be shut out to prevent distraction. With respect to the proportions of a room, they should be studied with reference to the table, which, as I have said, should in my opinion be of the size to accommodate not more than eight persons…

Perhaps it may be thought by many, that all these particulars are very immaterial, and that the consideration of them is very trifling; but my opinion is, that in all our actions, whether with reference to business or pleasure, it is a main point, in the first place, to produce a suitable disposition; and as dining is an occurrence of every day of our lives, or nearly so, and as our health and spirits depend in a great measure upon our vivid enjoyment of this our chief meal, it seems to me a more worthy object of study than those unreal occupations about which so many busy themselves in vain.

A Wery Good Notion of a Lunch

Charles Dickens (1812–1870) wrote his Pickwick Papers *(1837) in serial form. Mr Pickwick's fondness for food — and drink — is a running joke. Here his servant Sam Weller lays out a very acceptable feast after the hunt.*

'Weal pie,' said Mr Weller, soliloquising, as he arranged the eatables on the grass. 'Wery good thing is weal pie, when you know the lady as made it, and is quite sure it ain't kittens; and arter all though, where's the odds, when they're so like weal that the wery piemen themselves don't know the difference?'

'Don't they, Sam?' said Mr Pickwick.

'Not they, sir,' replied Mr Weller, touching his hat. 'I lodged in the same house vith a pieman once, sir, and a wery nice man he was — reg'lar clever chap, too — make pies out o' anything, he could. "What a number o' cats you keep, Mr Brooks," says I, when I'd got intimate with him. "Ah," says he, "I do — a good many," says he, "You must be wery fond o' cats," says I. "Other people is," says he, a-winkin' at me; "they ain't in season till the winter though," says he. "Not in season!" says I. "No," says he, "fruits is in, cats is out." "Why, what do you mean?" says I. "Mean?" says he. "That I'll never be a party to the combination o' the butchers, to keep up the price o' meat," says he. "Mr Weller," says he, a-squeezing my hand wery hard, and vispering in my ear — "don't mention this here agin — but it's the seasonin' as does it. They're all made o' them noble animals," says he, a-pointin' to a wery nice little tabby kitten, "and I seasons 'em for beefsteak, weal or kidney, 'cording to the demand."'

'He must have been a very ingenious young man, that, Sam,' said Mr Pickwick, with a slight shudder.

'Just was, sir,' replied Mr Weller, continuing his occupation of emptying the basket, 'and the pies was beautiful. Tongue —, well that's a wery good thing when it ain't a woman's. Bread, knuckle o' ham, reg'lar picter, cold beef in slices, wery good. What's in them stone jars, young touch-and-go?'

'Beer in this one,' replied the boy, taking from his shoulder a couple

of large stone bottles, fastened together by a leathern strap, 'cold punch in t'other.'

'And a wery good notion of a lunch it is, take it altogether,' said Mr Weller, surveying his arrangement of the repast with great satisfaction. 'Now, gen'l'm'n, "fall on," as the English said to the French when they fixed bagginets.' It needed no second invitation to induce the party to yield full justice to the meal; and as little pressing did it require to induce Mr Weller, the long gamekeeper, and the two boys, to station themselves on the grass, at a little distance, and do good execution upon a decent proportion of the viands. An old oak afforded a pleasant shelter to the group, and a rich prospect of arable and meadow land, intersected with luxuriant hedges, and richly ornamented with wood, lay spread out before them.

'This is delightful – thoroughly delightful!' said Mr Pickwick; the skin of whose expressive countenance was rapidly peeling off, with exposure to the sun.

'So it is – so it is, old fellow,' replied Wardle. 'Come, a glass of punch!'

'With great pleasure,' said Mr Pickwick, the satisfaction of whose countenance, after drinking it, bore testimony to the sincerity of the reply. 'Good,' said Mr Pickwick, smacking his lips. 'Very good. I'll take another. Cool, very cool. Come, gentlemen,' continued Mr Pickwick, still retaining his hold upon the jar, 'a toast. Our friends at Dingley Dell.' The toast was drunk with loud acclamations …

'Well, that certainly is most capital cold punch,' said Mr Pickwick, looking earnestly at the stone bottle; 'and the day is extremely warm, and – Tupman, my dear friend, a glass of punch?' 'With the greatest delight,' replied Mr Tupman; and having drank that glass, Mr Pickwick took another, just to see whether there was any orange peel in the punch, because orange peel always disagreed with him; and finding that there was not, Mr Pickwick took another glass to the health of their absent friend, and then felt himself imperatively called upon to propose another in honour of the punch-compounder, unknown.

This constant succession of glasses produced considerable effect upon Mr Pickwick; his countenance beamed with the most sunny smiles, laughter played around his lips, and good-humoured merriment twinkled in his eye. Yielding by degrees to the influence of the exciting liquid, rendered more so by the heat, Mr Pickwick expressed a strong desire to recollect a song which he had heard in his infancy, and the attempt proving abortive, sought to stimulate his memory with more glasses of punch, which appeared to have quite a contrary effect; for, from forgetting the words of the song, he began to forget how to articulate any words at all; and finally, after rising to his legs to address the company in an eloquent speech, he fell into the barrow, and fast asleep, simultaneously.

The basket having been repacked, and it being found perfectly impossible to awaken Mr Pickwick from his torpor, some discussion took place whether it would be better for Mr Weller to wheel his master back again, or to leave him where he was, until they should all be ready to return. The latter course was at length decided on; and as the further expedition was not to exceed an hour's duration, and as Mr Weller begged very hard to be one of the party, it was determined to leave Mr Pickwick asleep in the barrow, and to call for him on their return. So away they went, leaving Mr Pickwick snoring most comfortably in the shade.

✕ No Dust on the Mind

George Eliot (1819–1880) allows Arthur Donnithorne's planned breakfast confession to the rector to falter over cosiness and cold fowl in this extract from Adam Bede *(1859).*

The progress of civilization has made a breakfast or a dinner an easy and cheerful substitute for more troublesome and disagreeable ceremonies. We take a less gloomy view of our errors now our father confessor listens to us over his egg and coffee. We are more distinctly conscious that rude penances are out of the question for gentlemen in an enlightened age, and that mortal sin is not incompatible with an appetite for muffins. An assault on our pockets, which in more barbarous times would have been made in the brusque form of a pistol-shot, is quite a well-bred and smiling procedure now it has become a request for a loan thrown in as an easy parenthesis between the second and third glasses of claret.

Still, there was this advantage in the old rigid forms, that they committed you to the fulfilment of a resolution by some outward deed: when you have put your mouth to one end of a hole in a stone wall and are aware that there is an expectant ear at the other end, you are more likely to say what you came out with the intention of saying than if you were seated with your legs in an easy attitude under the mahogany with a companion who will have no reason to be surprised if you have nothing particular to say…

Arthur gave his horse to the groom at the rectory gate, and walked along the gravel towards the door which opened on the garden. He knew that the rector always breakfasted in his study, and the study lay on the left hand of this door, opposite the dining-room. It was a small low room, belonging to the old part of the house – dark with the sombre covers of the books that lined the walls; yet it looked very cheery this morning as Arthur reached the open window. For the morning sun fell aslant on the great glass globe with gold fish in it, which stood on a scagliola pillar in front of the ready-spread bachelor breakfast-table, and by the side of this breakfast-table was a group which would have made any room enticing.

In the crimson damask easy-chair sat Mr Irwine, with that radiant freshness which he always had when he came from his morning toilet; his finely formed plump white hand was playing along Juno's brown curly back; and close to Juno's tail, which was wagging with calm matronly pleasure, the two brown pups were rolling over each other in an ecstatic duet of worrying noises. On a cushion a little removed sat Pug, with the air of a maiden lady, who looked on these familiarities as animal weaknesses, which she made as little show as possible of observing. On the table, at Mr Irwine's elbow, lay the first volume of the Foulis Æschylus, which Arthur knew well by sight; and the silver coffee-pot, which Carroll was bringing in, sent forth a fragrant steam which completed the delights of a bachelor breakfast.

'Hallo, Arthur, that's a good fellow! You're just in time,' said Mr Irwine, as Arthur paused and stepped in over the low window-sill. 'Carroll, we shall want more coffee and eggs, and haven't you got some cold fowl for us to eat with that ham? Why, this is like old days, Arthur; you haven't been to breakfast with me these five years.'

'It was a tempting morning for a ride before breakfast,' said Arthur; 'and I used to like breakfasting with you so when I was reading with you. My grandfather is always a few degrees colder at breakfast than at any other hour in the day. I think his morning bath doesn't agree with him.' …

'I like breakfast-time better than any other moment in the day,' said Mr Irwine. 'No dust has settled on one's mind then, and it presents a clear mirror to the rays of things. I always have a favourite book by me at breakfast, and I enjoy the bits I pick up then so much, that regularly every morning it seems to me as if I should certainly become studious again.'

✕ The Mere Chink of Cups

Hospitality over the teacups has never been better described than by George Gissing (1857–1903), who in 1900 began a Fortnightly Review *serial called 'An Author at Grass', later published as* The Private Papers of Henry Ryecroft *(1903).*

One of the shining moments of my day is that when, having returned a little weary from an afternoon walk, I exchange boots for slippers, out-of-doors coat for easy, familiar, shabby jacket, and, in my deep, soft-elbowed chair, await the tea-tray.

Perhaps it is while drinking tea that I most of all enjoy the sense of leisure. In days gone by, I could but gulp down the refreshment, hurried, often harassed, by the thought of the work I had before me; often I was quite insensible of the aroma, the flavour, of what I drank. Now, how delicious is the soft yet penetrating odour which floats into my study, with the appearance of the teapot! What solace in the first cup, what deliberate sipping of that which follows! What a glow does it bring after a walk in chilly rain! The while, I look around at my books and pictures, tasting the happiness of their tranquil possession. I cast an eye towards my pipe; perhaps I prepare it, with seeming thoughtfulness, for the reception of tobacco. And never, surely, is tobacco more soothing, more suggestive of humane thoughts, than when it comes just after tea – itself a bland inspirer.

In nothing is the English genius for domesticity more notably declared than in the institution of this festival – almost one may call it so – of afternoon tea. Beneath simple roofs, the hour of tea has something in it of sacred; for it marks the end of domestic work and worry, the beginning of restful, sociable evening. The mere chink of cups and saucers tunes the mind to happy repose. I care nothing for your five o'clock tea of modish drawing-rooms, idle and wearisome like all else in which that world has part; I speak of tea where one is at home in quite another than the worldly sense. To admit mere strangers to your tea-table is profanation; on the other hand, English hospitality has here its kindliest aspect; never is friend more welcome than when he drops in for a cup of tea. Where tea is really a meal, with nothing between it and nine o'clock supper, it is – again in the true sense – the homeliest meal of the day. Is it believable that the Chinese, in who knows how many centuries, have derived from tea a millionth part of the pleasure or the good which it has brought to England in the past one hundred years?

I like to look at my housekeeper when she carries in the tray. Her mien is festal, yet in her smile there is a certain gravity, as though she performed an office which honoured her. She has dressed for the evening; that is to say, her clean and seemly attire of working hours is exchanged for garments suitable to fireside leisure; her cheeks are warm, for she has been making fragrant toast. Quickly her eye glances about my room, but only to have the pleasure of noting that all is in order; inconceivable that anything serious should need doing at this hour of the day. She brings the little table within the glow of the hearth, so that I can help myself without changing my easy position. If she speaks, it will only be a pleasant word or two; should she have anything important to say, the moment will be after tea, not before it; this she knows by instinct.

Perchance she may just stoop to sweep back a cinder which has fallen since, in my absence, she looked after the fire; it is done quickly and silently. Then, still smiling, she withdraws, and I know that she is going to enjoy her own tea, her own toast, in the warm, comfortable, sweet-smelling kitchen.

Not So Wild Wales

George Borrow (1803–1881) published Wild Wales: Its People, Language and Scenery *in 1862. It was inspired by a family holiday in Llangollen in 1854, and presented a much more romantic and enthusiastic view of the Welsh than was then customary. In search of the birthplace of the poet Goronwy Owen at Llanfair, Anglesey, he came across a hospitable miller.*

'Pray, gentleman, walk in!' said the miller; 'we are going to have our afternoon's meal, and shall be rejoiced if you will join us.'

'Yes, do, gentleman,' said the miller's wife, for such the good woman was; 'and many a welcome shall you have.'

I hesitated, and was about to excuse myself.

'Don't refuse, gentleman!' said both, 'surely you are not too proud to sit down with us?'

'I am afraid I shall only cause you trouble,' said I.

'Dim blinder, no trouble,' exclaimed both at once; 'pray do walk in!'

I entered the house, and the kitchen, parlour, or whatever it was, a nice little room with a slate floor. They made me sit down at a table by the window, which was already laid for a meal. There was a clean cloth upon it, a tea-pot, cups and saucers, a large plate of bread-and-butter, and a plate, on which were a few very thin slices of brown, watery cheese.

My good friends took their seats, the wife poured out tea for the stranger and her husband, helped us both to bread-and-butter and the watery cheese, then took care of herself. Before, however, I could taste the tea, the wife, seeming to recollect herself, started up, and hurrying to a cupboard, produced a basin full of snow-white lump sugar, and taking the spoon out of my hand, placed two of the largest lumps in my cup, though she helped neither her husband nor herself; the sugar-basin being probably only kept for grand occasions.

My eyes filled with tears; for in the whole course of my life I had never experienced so much genuine hospitality. Honour to the miller of Mona and his wife; and honour to the kind hospitable Celts in general!

✗ Mrs Hudson Rises to the Occasion

Sir Arthur Conan Doyle (1859–1930) makes Mrs Hudson serve up an unusual but most welcome breakfast dish ('The Adventure of the Naval Treaty', 1893).

'You are not wounded, Holmes?' I asked, as my friend entered the room.

'Tut, it is only a scratch through my own clumsiness,' he answered, nodding his good-mornings to us. 'This case of yours, Mr Phelps, is certainly one of the darkest which I have ever investigated.'

'I feared that you would find it beyond you.'

'It has been a most remarkable experience.'

'That bandage tells of adventures,' said I. 'Won't you tell us what has happened?'

'After breakfast, my dear Watson. Remember that I have breathed thirty miles of Surrey air this morning. I suppose that there has been no answer from my cabman advertisement? Well, well, we cannot expect to score every time.'

The table was all laid, and just as I was about to ring, Mrs Hudson entered with the tea and coffee. A few minutes later she brought in three covers, and we all drew up to the table, Holmes ravenous, I curious, and Phelps in the gloomiest state of depression.

'Mrs Hudson has risen to the occasion,' said Holmes, uncovering a dish of curried chicken. 'Her cuisine is a little limited, but she has as good an idea of breakfast as a Scotch-woman. What have you here, Watson?'

'Ham and eggs,' I answered.

'Good! What are you going to take, Mr Phelps – curried fowl or eggs, or will you help yourself?'

'Thank you. I can eat nothing,' said Phelps.

'Oh, come! Try the dish before you.'

'Thank you, I would really rather not.'

'Well, then,' said Holmes, with a mischievous twinkle, 'I suppose that you have no objection to helping me?'

Phelps raised the cover, and as he did so he uttered a scream, and sat there staring with a face as white as the plate upon which he looked.

Across the centre of it was lying a little cylinder of blue-gray paper. He caught it up, devoured it with his eyes, and then danced madly about the room, pressing it to his bosom and shrieking out in his delight. Then he fell back into an arm-chair so limp and exhausted with his own emotions that we had to pour brandy down his throat to keep him from fainting.

'There! there!' said Holmes, soothing, patting him upon the shoulder. 'It was too bad to spring it on you like this, but Watson here will tell you that I never can resist a touch of the dramatic.'

Phelps seized his hand and kissed it. 'God bless you!' he cried. 'You have saved my honour.'

'Well, my own was at stake, you know,' said Holmes. 'I assure you it is just as hateful to me to fail in a case as it can be to you to blunder over a commission.'

Phelps thrust away the precious document into the innermost pocket of his coat.

'I have not the heart to interrupt your breakfast any further, and yet I am dying to know how you got it and where it was.'

Sherlock Holmes swallowed a cup of coffee, and turned his attention to the ham and eggs. Then he rose, lit his pipe, and settled himself down into his chair.

The Real Ally Daly

James Joyce (1882–1941) invested his A Portrait of the Artist as a Young Man *(1916) with personal memories: here Stephen Dedalus recalls his first Christmas dinner with the grown-ups.*

A great fire, banked high and red, flamed in the grate and under the ivy-twined branches of the chandelier the Christmas table was spread. They had come home a little late and still dinner was not ready: but it would be ready in a jiffy his mother had said. They were waiting for the door to open and for the servants to come in, holding the big dishes covered with their heavy metal covers …

Mr Dedalus dropped his coat-tails and went over to the sideboard. He brought forth a great stone jar of whisky from the locker and filled the decanter slowly, bending now and then to see how much he had poured in. Then replacing the jar in the locker he poured a little of the whisky into two glasses, added a little water and came back with them to the fireplace.

–A thimbleful, John, he said, just to whet your appetite …

The servants entered and placed the dishes on the table. Mrs Dedalus followed and the places were arranged.

–Sit over, she said.

Mr Dedalus went to the end of the table and said:

–Now, Mrs Riordan, sit over. John, sit you down, my hearty.

He looked round to where Uncle Charles sat and said:

–Now then, sir, there's a bird here waiting for you.

When all had taken their seats he laid his hand on the cover and then said quickly, withdrawing it:

–Now, Stephen.

Stephen stood up in his place to say the grace before meals:

–Bless us O Lord, and these Thy gifts which through Thy bounty we are about to receive through Christ, the Lord, Amen.

All blessed themselves and Mr Dedalus with a sigh of pleasure lifted from the dish the heavy cover pearled around the edge with glittering drops.

Stephen looked at the plump turkey which had lain, trussed and

skewered, on the kitchen table. He knew that his father had paid a guinea for it in Dunn's of D'Olier Street and that the man had prodded it often at the breastbone to show how good it was; and he remembered the man's voice when he said:

—Take that one sir. That's the real Ally Daly.

Why did Mr Barrett at Clongowes call his pandybat a turkey? But Clongowes was far away: and the warm heavy smell of turkey and ham and celery rose from the plates and dishes and the great fire was banked high and red in the grate and the green ivy and red holly made you feel so happy and when dinner was ended the big plum pudding would be carried in, studded with peeled almonds and sprigs of holly, with bluish fire running around it and a little green flag flying from the top.

It was his first Christmas dinner and he thought of his little brothers and sisters who were waiting in the nursery, as he had often waited, till the pudding came. The deep low collar and the Eton jacket made him feel queer and oldish: and that morning when his mother had brought him down to the parlour, dressed for mass, his father had cried. That was because he was thinking of his own father. And Uncle Charles had said so too.

Mr Dedalus covered the dish and began to eat hungrily.

✗ The Ultimate in Thoughtfulness

In an essay otherwise devoted to observations of flowers and fauna, Richard Jefferies (1848–1887) suddenly breaks off to recall a remarkable instance of hospitality ('The Haunt of the Hare', The Open Air, *1885).*

One day in autumn, after toiling with their guns, which are heavy in the September heats, across the fields and over the hills, the hospitable owner of the place suddenly asked his weary and thirsty friend which he would have, champagne, ale, or spirits. They were just then in the midst of a cover, the trees kept off the wind, the afternoon sun was warm, and thirst very natural. They had not been shooting in the cover, but had to pass through to other cornfields. It seemed a sorry jest to ask which would be preferred in that lonely and deserted spot, miles from home or any house whence refreshment could be obtained – wine, spirits, or ale? – an absurd question, and irritating under the circumstances. As it was repeated persistently, however, the reply was at length given, in no very good humour, and wine chosen. Forthwith putting down his gun, the interrogator pushed in among the underwood, and from a cavity concealed beneath some bushes drew forth a bottle of champagne. He had several of these stores hidden in various parts of the domain, ready whichever way the chance of sport should direct their footsteps.

✕ A Party Round a Table

Virginia Woolf (1882–1941) made her novel To the Lighthouse *(1927) a eulogy to her mother: here she recalls the atmosphere around the family dinner table and the glory of a slow-cooked French* daube *three decades before Elizabeth David sang its praises.*

Now eight candles were stood down the table, and after the first stoop the flames stood upright and drew with them into visibility the long table entire, and in the middle a yellow and purple dish of fruit. What had she done with it, Mrs Ramsay wondered, for Rose's arrangement of the grapes and pears, of the horny pink-lined shell, of the bananas, made her think of a trophy fetched from the bottom of the sea, of Neptune's banquet, of the bunch that hangs with vine leaves over the shoulder of Bacchus (in some picture), among the leopard skins and the torches lolloping red and gold …

Now all the candles were lit up, and the faces on both sides of the table were brought nearer by the candle light, and composed, as they had not been in the twilight, into a party round a table, for the night was now shut off by panes of glass, which, far from giving any accurate view of the outside world, rippled it so strangely that here, inside the room, seemed to be order and dry land; there, outside, a reflection in which things waved and vanished, waterily.

Some change at once went through them all, as if this had really happened, and they were all conscious of making a party together in a hollow, on an island; had their common cause against that fluidity out there …

An exquisite scent of olives and oil and juice rose from the great brown dish as Marthe, with a little flourish, took the cover off. The cook had spent three days over that dish. And she must take great care, Mrs Ramsay thought, diving into the soft mass, to choose a specially tender piece for William Bankes. And she peered into the dish, with its shiny walls and its confusion of savoury brown and yellow meats and its bay leaves and its wine, and thought, This will celebrate the occasion – a curious sense rising in her, at once freakish and tender, of celebrating a festival, as if two emotions were called up in her, one

profound – for what could be more serious than the love of man for woman, what more commanding, more impressive, bearing in its bosom the seeds of death; at the same time these lovers, these people entering into illusion glittering-eyed, must be danced round with mockery, decorated with garlands.

'It is a triumph,' said Mr Bankes, laying his knife down for a moment. He had eaten attentively. It was rich; it was tender. It was perfectly cooked. How did she manage these things in the depths of the country? he asked her. She was a wonderful woman. All his love, all his reverence, had returned; and she knew it.

'It is a French recipe of my grandmother's,' said Mrs Ramsay, speaking with a ring of great pleasure in her voice. Of course it was French. What passes for cookery in England is an abomination (they agreed). It is putting cabbages in water. It is roasting meat till it is like leather. It is cutting off the delicious skins of vegetables. 'In which,' said Mr Bankes, 'all the virtue of the vegetable is contained.' And the waste, said Mrs Ramsay. A whole French family could live on what an English cook throws away.

2 Dazzling All Beholders

Here enter you, and welcome from our hearts,
All noble sparks, endowed with gallant parts.
This is the glorious place, which bravely shall
Afford wherewith to entertain you all.

Inscription on the gates of the Abbey of Thelema,
in *Pantagruel* by François Rabelais, 1532

When times are bad, people like to lose
themselves in the sheer glamour of another
period: beautiful wardrobes, magnificent meals
served in elegant settings.

Shirley MacLaine on playing Martha Levinson
in 'Downton Abbey'

1

Make the Ladies to Skip and Shriek

Robert May (1588–c.1664) published The Accomplisht Cook *in 1660. In a section called 'Triumphs and Trophies in Cookery, to be used at Festival Times, as Twelfth-day' he offered spectacularly playful recipes, including one for pies filled with live birds and frogs, and pastry cannons that really fired.*

Make the likeness of a Ship in Paste-board, with Flags and Streamers, the Guns belonging to it of Kickses [hollow straws], bind them about with packthread, and cover them with close paste proportionable to the fashion of a Cannon with Carriages, lay them in places convenient as you see them in Ships of war, with such holes and trains of powder that they may all take Fire.

Place your Ship firm in the great Charger; then make a salt round about it, and stick therein egg-shells full of sweet water, you may by a great Pin take all the meat out of the egg by blowing, and then fill it up with the rose-water, then in another Charger have the proportion of a Stag made of coarse paste, with a broad Arrow in the side of him, and his body filled up with claret-wine; in another Charger at the end of the Stag have the proportion of a Castle with Battlements, Portcullises, Gates and Draw-Bridges made of Paste-board, the Guns and Kickses, and covered with coarse paste as the former; place it at a distance from the ship to fire at each other.

At each side of the Charger wherein is the Stag, place a Pie made of course [sic] paste, in one of which let there be some live Frogs, in the other some live Birds; make these Pies of course [sic] Paste filled with bran, and yellowed over with saffron or the yolks of eggs, gild them over in spots, as also the Stag, the Ship, and Castle; bake them, and place them with gilt bay-leaves on turrets and tunnels of the Castle and Pies; being baked, make a hole in the bottom of your Pies, take out the bran, put in your Frogs, and Birds, and close up the holes with the same coarse paste, then cut the Lids neatly up …

Before you fire the trains of powder, order it so that some of the Ladies may be persuaded to pluck the Arrow out of the Stag, then will the Claret-wine follow, as blood that runneth out of a wound.

By degrees fire the trains of each side. This done, to sweeten the stink of powder, let the Ladies take the egg-shells full of sweet waters and throw them at each other.

All dangers being seemingly over, by this time you may suppose they will desire to see what is in the pies; where lifting first the lid off one pie, out skip some Frogs, which make the Ladies to skip and shriek; next after the other pie, whence come out the Birds, who by a natural instinct flying in the light, will put out the Candles; so that what with the flying Birds and skipping Frogs, the one above, the other beneath, will cause much delight and pleasure to the whole company.

These were formerly the delight of the Nobility, before good House-keeping had left England, and the Sword really acted that which was only counterfeited in such honest and laudable Exercises as these.

✕ The Epicure

In his 1610 play The Alchemist, *Ben Jonson (1572–1637) uses Sir Epicure Mammon's description of his dining habits to satirise gourmet excesses.*

My meat shall all come in, in Indian shells,
Dishes of agate set in gold, and studded
With emeralds, sapphires, hyacinths, and rubies.
The tongues of carps, dormice, and camels' heels,
Boil'd in the spirit of sol, and dissolv'd pearl,
Apicius' diet, 'gainst the epilepsy:
And I will eat these broths with spoons of amber,
Headed with diamond and carbuncle.
My foot-boy shall eat pheasants, calver'd salmons,
Knots, godwits, lampreys: I myself will have
The beards of barbels served, instead of salads;
Oil'd mushrooms; and the swelling unctuous paps
Of a fat pregnant sow, newly cut off,
Drest with an exquisite, and poignant sauce;
For which, I'll say unto my cook, There's gold,
Go forth, and be a knight.

✕ The Company of the Saucepan

In his Lives of the Most Excellent Painters, Sculptors and Architects *(1550), Giorgio Vasari (1511–1574) describes the culinary high jinks of the Florentine sculptor Giovanni Rustici and his fellow 'Companions of the Saucepan'.*

There used to assemble in his rooms a number of good fellows called the Company of the Saucepan, which was limited to twelve members, and each one of the twelve might bring four and no more to their suppers. And each one was bound to bring something to the supper made with skill and invention, and when he came he presented it to the master of the feast, who handed it on to any one he liked.

One evening when Rustici was giving a supper to his Company of the Saucepan, he ordered that, instead of a table, a great kettle or saucepan should be made out of a wine vat, and they all sat inside it, and it was lighted from the handle which was over their heads. And when they were all comfortably settled, there rose up in the middle a tree with many branches bearing the supper, that is, the food on plates. And then it descended again and brought up a second course, and afterwards a third, and so on, while there were servants going round with precious wines and musicians playing below. This was greatly praised by the men of the Company.

Rustici's dish that time was a cauldron made of pastry, in which Ulysses was dipping his father to make him young again. The two figures were capons with their limbs arranged to make them look like men.

Andrea del Sarto, who was one of the Company, presented a temple with eight sides, like S. Giovanni, but resting on columns. The pavement was of gelatine, like different coloured mosaics; the pillars, which looked like porphyry, were great sausages, the base and capitals of Parmesan cheese, the cornices of sugar, and the tribunes of marchpane. In the middle was placed the choir desk of cold veal, with a book of macaroni paste, having the letters and notes for singing made with peppercorns, and those who were singing were thrushes with their beaks open and wearing little surplices, and behind these for the bassi were two fat pigeons, with six ortolans for the soprani.

Spillo, another member, brought the model of a smith, made of a great goose, or some such bird, with all the tools for mending the saucepan if it were necessary. Domenico Puligo brought a roast pig, made to represent a girl with her distaff by her side watching a brood of chickens. The other things represented were also very good, but we cannot tell them one by one.

Toasts on the Nail

Jacobean feasts involved elaborate toasting, explained Thomas Wright (1810–1877) in The Homes of Other Days *(1871). The 'little book' he quotes is by Thomas Middleton, who goes on to say that the next toast should be to 'his Lady of little worth, or peradventure to his light-hele'd mistress.'*

One of the great characteristics of the dinner-table at this period was the formality of drinking, especially that of drinking healths, so much cried down by the Puritans. This formality was enforced with great strictness and ceremony. It was not exactly the modern practice of giving a toast, but each person in turn rose, named some one to whom he individually drank (not one of the persons present), and emptied his cup. 'He that begins the health,' we are told in a little book published in 1623, 'first uncovering his head, he takes a full cup in his hand, and setting his countenance with a grave aspect, he craves for audience; silence being once obtained, he begins to breathe out the name, peradventure, of some honourable personage, whose health is drunk to, and he that pledges must likewise off with his cap, kiss his fingers, and bow himself in sign of a reverent acceptance. When the leader sees his follower thus prepared, he sups up his broth, turns the bottom of the cup upward, and, in ostentation of his dexterity, gives the cup a phillip [flip] to make it cry "twango". And thus the first scene is acted. The cup being newly replenished to the breadth of a hair, he that is the pledger must now begin his part; and thus it goes round throughout the whole company.' In order to ascertain that each person had fairly drunk off his cup, in turning it up he was to pour all that remained in it on his nail, and if there were too much to remain as a drop on the nail without running off, he was made to drink his cup full again. This was termed drinking on the nail, for which convivialists invented a mock Latin phrase, and called it drinking super-nagulum, or super-naculum.

✂ Sancho Panza's Skimmings

The wedding feast of Camacho the Rich and Quiteria the Fair became a byword for gastronomic excess (Miguel de Cervantes, Don Quixote*, 1615, translated by John Ormsby in 1885).*

The first thing that presented itself to Sancho's eyes was a whole ox spitted on a whole elm tree, and in the fire at which it was to be roasted there was burning a middling-sized mountain of faggots, and six stewpots that stood round the blaze had not been made in the ordinary mould of common pots, for they were six half wine-jars, each fit to hold the contents of a slaughter-house; they swallowed up whole sheep and hid them away in their insides without showing any more sign of them than if they were pigeons. Countless were the hares ready skinned and the plucked fowls that hung on the trees for burial in the pots, numberless the wildfowl and game of various sorts suspended from the branches that the air might keep them cool.

Sancho counted more than sixty wine skins of over six gallons each, and all filled, as it proved afterwards, with generous wines. There were, besides, piles of the whitest bread, like the heaps of corn one sees on the threshing-floors. There was a wall made of cheeses arranged like open brick-work, and two cauldrons full of oil, bigger than those of a dyer's shop, served for cooking fritters, which when fried were taken out with two mighty shovels, and plunged into another cauldron of prepared honey that stood close by. Of cooks and cook-maids there were over fifty, all clean, brisk, and blithe.

In the capacious belly of the ox were a dozen soft little sucking-pigs, which, sewn up there, served to give it tenderness and flavour. The spices of different kinds did not seem to have been bought by the pound but by the quarter, and all lay open to view in a great chest. In short, all the preparations made for the wedding were in rustic style, but abundant enough to feed an army.

Sancho observed all, contemplated all, and everything won his heart. The first to captivate and take his fancy were the pots, out of which he would have very gladly helped himself to a moderate pipkinful; then the wine skins secured his affections; and lastly, the produce of the frying-pans, if, indeed, such imposing cauldrons may be called frying-pans; and unable to control himself or bear it any longer, he approached one of the busy cooks and civilly but hungrily begged permission to soak a scrap of bread in one of the pots; to which the cook made answer,

'Brother, this is not a day on which hunger is to have any sway, thanks to the rich Camacho; get down and look about for a ladle and skim off a hen or two, and much good may they do you.'

'I don't see one,' said Sancho.

'Wait a bit,' said the cook; 'sinner that I am! how particular and bashful you are!' and so saying, he seized a bucket and plunging it into one of the half jars took up three hens and a couple of geese, and said to Sancho, 'Fall to, friend, and take the edge off your appetite with these skimmings until dinner-time comes.'

'I have nothing to put them in,' said Sancho.

'Well then,' said the cook, 'take spoon and all; for Camacho's wealth and happiness furnish everything.'

✗ If I Were a Rich Man …

Gastronomy, or The Bon-Vivant's Guide, *first published in 1801, was trans-*
lated from the French of the poet and humorist Joseph Berchoux (1760–1838)
in 1810. Berchoux is credited with coining the word 'gastronomy'. Here he
jokingly fantasises on his ideal feast. Sillery is a champagne; Perigueux pie
is flavoured with truffles. Notice the snide reference to his contemporary, the
English cook Hannah Glasse.

Should Plutus, my friends! Whom I daily implore,
Ever grant me five thousand *per annum*, or more;
To social enjoyment my thoughts I'll devote,
And my own, by your happiness, strive to promote.
No more will we part, and the table we love
Shall the centre and bond of our amity prove.
With wines of choice flavour, my cellars I'll stock;
Grave, sillery, *clos de cougeaux*, and old hock.
To me shall each dainty be constantly sent,
Which nature produces, or art can invent;
Turtle, turbot, and dory, the Perigueux pie,
Quails, ortolans, grouse, and the ptarmigan shy:
Whilst my hot-houses, proof against frost, hail or snow,
Pines, grapes and green peas, shall, at Christmas, bestow.
Though, dame Glasse! from your book, there's not much to be got,
Still your maxim is good – 'Serve the dinner up, hot,'
In this I'm forestall'd, for, the choicest ragout,

If cold when you eat it, is not worth a sous.
The taste of your numerous friends ascertain,
And let none, of the least inattention, complain.
Remember the parts which they each think the best;
A leg, one prefers, and another the breast.
'Tis the wing, of a chicken, the ladies most like;
Give the white side of turbot, the back of a pike.
With neatness and justice the slices dispense,
Nor, from interest, rank, or some other pretence,
All a favourite part, on one only, bestow;
For, if ever equality reign, here below,
Round a plentiful board we enjoy its delights,
Where, as children of Comus, all claim equal rights …

When dinner's announced, to all business a truce;
Ne'er a sad, or e'en serious point introduce;
Our rulers should punish intrusion, by fines,
And nothing disturb a good-fellow, who dines.
To accomplish a total exclusion of care,
The gifts of the ivy-crown'd god you must share;
With burgundy, richly empurple your lip,
Or, in rosy champaign, wit and pleasantry sip.
But be not seduced, here to quicken your speed;
Tow'rds the summit of ecstasy, slowly proceed:
An ample dessert, in reserve we retain,
If I, then, am too cautious, you've leave to complain.

✕ All Mingled Higgledy-Piggledy

Washington Irving (1783–1859) describes a sensual harvest feast in the Dutch style in his 'Legend of Sleepy Hollow'. The frequently mentioned pumpkins are a key part of the gothic tale's dramatic climax.

As Ichabod jogged slowly on his way, his eye, ever open to every symptom of culinary abundance, ranged with delight over the treasures of jolly autumn. On all sides he beheld vast store of apples; some hanging in oppressive opulence on the trees; some gathered into baskets and barrels for the market; others heaped up in rich piles for the cider-press. Farther on he beheld great fields of Indian corn, with its golden ears peeping from their leafy coverts, and holding out the promise of cakes and hasty pudding; and the yellow pumpkins lying beneath them, turning up their fair round bellies to the sun, and giving ample prospects of the most luxurious of pies; and anon he passed the fragrant buckwheat fields, breathing the odor of the beehive, and as he beheld them, soft anticipations stole over his mind of dainty slapjacks, well buttered, and garnished with honey or treacle, by the delicate little dimpled hand of Katrina Van Tassel.

Thus feeding his mind with many sweet thoughts and 'sugared suppositions', he journeyed along the sides of a range of hills which look out upon some of the goodliest scenes of the mighty Hudson …

It was toward evening that Ichabod arrived at the castle of the Heer Van Tassel, which he found thronged with the pride and flower of the adjacent country. Old farmers, a spare leathern-faced race, in home-spun coats and breeches, blue stockings, huge shoes, and magnificent pewter buckles. Their brisk withered little dames, in close crimped caps, long-waisted short-gowns, home-spun petticoats, with scissors and pincushions, and gay calico pockets hanging on the outside. Buxom lasses, almost as antiquated as their mothers, excepting where a straw hat, a fine ribbon, or perhaps a white frock, gave symptoms of city innovation. The sons, in short square-skirted coats with rows of stupendous brass buttons, and their hair generally queued in the fashion of the times, especially if they could procure an eel-skin for the purpose, it being esteemed, throughout the country, as a potent nourisher and strengthener of the hair …

Fain would I pause to dwell upon the world of charms that burst upon the enraptured gaze of my hero, as he entered the state parlour of Van Tassel's mansion. Not those of the bevy of buxom lasses, with their luxurious display of red and white; but the ample charms of a genuine Dutch country tea-table, in the sumptuous time of autumn. Such heaped-up platters of cakes of various and almost indescribable kinds, known only to experienced Dutch housewives! There was the doughty dough-nut, the tenderer *oly koek* [oilseed cake], and the crisp and crumbling cruller; sweet cakes and short cakes, ginger cakes and honey cakes, and the whole family of cakes.

And then there were apple pies and peach pies and pumpkin pies; besides slices of ham and smoked beef; and moreover delectable dishes of preserved plums, and peaches, and pears, and quinces; not to mention broiled shad and roasted chickens; together with bowls of milk and cream, all mingled higgledy-piggledy, pretty much as I have enumerated them, with the motherly tea-pot sending up its clouds of vapour from the midst – Heaven bless the mark! I want breath and time to discuss this banquet as it deserves, and am too eager to get on with my story. Happily, Ichabod Crane was not in so great a hurry as his historian, but did ample justice to every dainty.

✕ Quails Decked in Their Plumage

Gustave Flaubert (1821–1880) makes the grand dinner party to which Emma and Charles Bovary are invited by a grateful aristocratic patient the catalyst of Emma's dissatisfaction with her provincial world (Madame Bovary, 1856).

At seven o'clock dinner was served. The men, who were in the majority, were seated at the first table, in the vestibule; the ladies at the second, in the dining-room, with the Marquis and the Marquise.

Emma felt on entering as though she were swathed about with warm air, blended of the perfume of flowers and fine linen, the savour of viands and the delicate odour of truffles. The flambeaux in the candelabra were mirrored in long tongues of light in the silver dish-covers. The facets of the cut glass, veiled by a softening mist, radiated a delicate glimmer; down the whole table's length were floral bouquets ranged in line, and on the wide-rimmed plates stood napkins folded like bishops' mitres, each holding in its opening a little oval roll. Lobsters protruded their red claws over the dish's edge. There were masses of splendid fruit piled on moss in filigree baskets; quails decked in their plumage. It was a medley of fragrant odours. In silk stockings, knee breeches, white stock and frilled shirt, the major-domo, solemn as a judge, handed the dishes between the shoulders of the guests, and with a magic twist of his spoon caused the morsel of your choice to leap on to your plate. On the high porcelain stove, with its copper rods, stood the statue of a woman draped to the chin, looking calmly down on the thronged apartment.

Madame Bovary noticed that a number of ladies had not put their gloves in their glasses.

At the top end of the table, alone among the crowd of women, bending down over a well-filled plate, with his napkin tied round his neck like a child's bib, sat an old man, who, as he ate, let little drops of gravy trickle from his mouth. His eyes were weak and watery, and he wore a little pigtail tied with a bow of black ribbon. He was the Marquis's father-in-law, the old Duc de Laverdière, the quondam favourite of the Comte d'Artois, in the old hunting days at Vaudreuil at the Marquis de Conflans's. The gossips said he had been one of Marie Antoinette's lovers, coming between Messieurs de Coigny and de Lauzun. He had led a tumultuous and dissolute life, crammed full of duels and gambling and abductions. He had got through all his money, and had been the terror of his family. A footman, stationed behind his chair, would lean down and bawl into his ear the names of the several dishes, and with stammering tongue and trembling fingers he would indicate the one he desired.

Try as she would, Emma simply could not keep her eyes off the old man and his drooping lips. She gazed at him as though he were some extraordinary phenomenon, something august. He had lived at Court and shared the couch of Queens!

The glasses were filled with iced champagne. Emma felt a thrill go through her as she tasted the coldness of it in her mouth. She had never seen a pomegranate or eaten a pineapple. The very caster sugar seemed whiter here, and more finely powdered, than elsewhere.

✖ Our Arabian Nights Plates

Marcel Proust (1871–1922) describes this evening meal at Combray in the first part of his À la recherche du temps perdu (1913–1927). It was translated by CK Scott Moncrieff as Swann's Way (1922).

We would still be found seated in front of our Arabian Nights plates, weighed down by the heat of the day, and even more by our heavy meal. For upon the permanent foundation of eggs, cutlets, potatoes, preserves, and biscuits, whose appearance on the table she no longer announced to us, Françoise would add – as the labour of fields and orchards, the harvest of the tides, the luck of the markets, the kindness of neighbours, and her own genius might provide; and so effectively that our bill of fare, like the quatrefoils that were carved on the porches of cathedrals in the thirteenth century, reflected to some extent the march of the seasons and the incidents of human life – a brill, because the fish-woman had guaranteed its freshness; a turkey, because she had seen a beauty in the market at Roussainville-le-Pin; cardoons with marrow, because she had never done them for us in that way before; a roast leg of mutton, because the fresh air made one hungry and there would be plenty of time for it to 'settle down' in the seven hours before dinner; spinach, by way of a change; apricots, because they were still hard to get; gooseberries, because in another fortnight there would be none left; raspberries, which M. Swann had brought specially; cherries, the first to come from the cherry-tree, which had yielded none for the last two years; a cream cheese, of which in those days I was extremely fond; an almond cake, because she had ordered one the evening before; a fancy loaf, because it was our turn to 'offer' the holy bread.

And when all these had been eaten, a work composed expressly for ourselves, but dedicated more particularly to my father, who had a fondness for such things, a cream of chocolate, inspired in the mind, created by the hand of Françoise, would be laid before us, light and fleeting as an 'occasional piece' of music, into which she had poured the whole of her talent. Anyone who refused to partake of it, saying: 'No, thank you, I have finished; I am not hungry,' would at once have been lowered to the level of the Philistines who, when an artist makes

them a present of one of his works, examine its weight and material, whereas what is of value is the creator's intention and his signature. To have left even the tiniest morsel in the dish would have shewn as much discourtesy as to rise and leave a concert hall while the 'piece' was still being played, and under the composer's very eyes.

Men and Girls Came and Went Like Moths

F Scott Fitzgerald (1896–1940) wrote The Great Gatsby *(1925) as a portrait of the mixture of decadence and idealism typical of the Jazz Age.*

There was music from my neighbour's house through the summer nights. In his blue gardens men and girls came and went like moths among the whisperings and the champagne and the stars. At high tide in the afternoon I watched his guests diving from the tower of his raft, or taking the sun on the hot sand of his beach while his two motor-boats slit the waters of the Sound, drawing aquaplanes over cataracts of foam. On week-ends his Rolls-Royce became an omnibus, bearing parties to and from the city between nine in the morning and long past midnight, while his station wagon scampered like a brisk yellow bug to meet all trains. And on Mondays eight servants, including an extra gardener, toiled all day with mops and scrubbing-brushes and hammers and garden-shears, repairing the ravages of the night before.

Every Friday five crates of oranges and lemons arrived from a fruiterer in New York – every Monday these same oranges and lemons left his back door in a pyramid of pulpless halves. There was a machine in the kitchen which could extract the juice of two hundred oranges in half an hour if a little button was pressed two hundred times by a butler's thumb.

At least once a fortnight a corps of caterers came down with several hundred feet of canvas and enough colored lights to make a Christmas tree of Gatsby's enormous garden. On buffet tables, garnished with glistening hors-d'oeuvre, spiced baked hams crowded against salads of harlequin designs and pastry pigs and turkeys bewitched to a dark gold. In the main hall a bar with a real brass rail was set up, and stocked with gins and liquors and with cordials so long forgotten that most of his female guests were too young to know one from another …

There was dancing now on the canvas in the garden; old men pushing young girls backward in eternal graceless circles, superior couples holding each other tortuously, fashionably, and keeping in the corners – and a great number of single girls dancing individualistically or relieving the orchestra for a moment of the burden of the banjo or the traps.

3 Love Bites

Men are like fires. If you don't feed them,
they go out.

Mae West

My weaknesses have always been food
and men — in that order.

Dolly Parton

✄ Flaunting It

In his Natural History, *Pliny the Elder (AD 23–79) relates the magnificent way in which Cleopatra, Queen of Egypt, entertained the bedazzled Roman consul Mark Antony when he visited her in Alexandria in 41 BC. This 1855 translation is by John Bostock.*

There were formerly two pearls, the largest that had been ever seen in the whole world: Cleopatra, the last of the queens of Egypt, was in possession of them both, they having come to her by descent from the kings of the East. When Antony had been sated by her, day after day, with the most exquisite banquets, this queenly courtesan, inflated with vanity and disdainful arrogance, affected to treat all this sumptuousness and all these vast preparations with the greatest contempt; upon which Antony enquired what there was that could possibly be added to such extraordinary magnificence. To this she made answer, that on a single entertainment she would expend ten millions of sesterces. Antony was extremely desirous to learn how that could be done, but looked upon it as a thing quite impossible; and a wager was the result.

On the following day, upon which the matter was to be decided, in order that she might not lose the wager, she had an entertainment set before Antony, magnificent in every respect, though no better than his usual repast. Upon this, Antony joked with her, and enquired what was the amount expended upon it; to which she made answer that the banquet which he then beheld was only a trifling appendage to the real banquet, and that she alone would consume at the meal to the ascertained value of that amount, she herself would swallow the ten millions of sesterces; and so ordered the second course to be served. In obedience to her instructions, the servants placed before her a single vessel, which was filled with vinegar, a liquid, the sharpness and strength of which is able to dissolve pearls. At this moment she was wearing in her ears those choicest and most rare and unique produc- tions of Nature; and while Antony was waiting to see what she was going to do, taking one of them from out of her ear, she threw it into the vinegar, and directly it was melted, swallowed it. Lucius Plancus, who had been named umpire in the wager, placed his hand upon the other at the very instant that she was making preparations to dissolve it in a similar manner, and declared that Antony had lost – an omen which, in the result, was fully confirmed.

The fame of the second pearl is equal to that which attends its fellow. After the queen, who had thus come off victorious on so important a question, had been seized [much later, by Octavian's men], it was cut asunder, in order that this, the other half of the entertainment, might serve as pendants for the ears of Venus, in the Pantheon at Rome.

✕ Feasting On Your Sight

William Shakespeare (c. 1564–1616) is doubtful as to the effect of drink on love ('it provokes the desire but takes away the performance', says the porter in Macbeth*), but he enjoys playing with tasty metaphors in Sonnet 75.*

So are you to my thoughts as food to life,
Or as sweet-seasoned showers are to the ground;
And for the peace of you I hold such strife
As 'twixt a miser and his wealth is found;
Now proud as an enjoyer and anon
Doubting the filching age will steal his treasure,
Now counting best to be with you alone,
Then bettered that the world may see my pleasure.
Sometime all full with feasting on your sight,
And by and by clean starvèd for a look;
Possessing or pursuing no delight,
Save what is had or must from you be took.
Thus do I pine and surfeit day by day,
Or gluttoning on all, or all away.

✕ An Hellespont of Cream

For John Davies of Hereford, writing in 1598, cream rather than ale was the route to his mistress's side.

If there were, O! an Hellespont of cream
Between us, milk-white Mistress, I would swim
To you, to show to both my love's extreme,
Leander-like, – yea, dive from brim to brim.
But met I with a butter'd pippin-pie
Floating upon't, that would I make my boat,
To waft me to you without jeopardy:
Though sea-sick I might be while it did float.
Yet if a storm should rise, by night or day,
Of sugar snows or hail of care-aways,
Then if I found a pancake in my way,
It like a plank should bear me to your quays,
Which having found, if they tobacco kept,
The smoke should dry me well before I slept.

✕ A Volley of Small Charms

In his picaresque novel Tom Jones *(1749), Henry Fielding (1707–1754) created a dinnertime seduction scene between Tom and Mrs Waters which became cinema legend in Tony Richardson's 1963 film starring Albert Finney and Joyce Redman.*

We think it no disparagement to our hero to mention the immoderate ardour with which he laid about him at this season. Indeed, it may be doubted whether Ulysses, who by the way seems to have had the best stomach of all the heroes in that eating poem of the Odyssey, ever made a better meal. Three pounds at least of that flesh which formerly had contributed to the composition of an ox was now honoured with becoming part of the individual Mr Jones. This particular we thought ourselves obliged to mention, as it may account for our hero's temporary neglect of his fair companion, who eat but very little, and was indeed employed in considerations of a very different nature …

What were the weapons now used to captivate the heart of Mr Jones? First, from two lovely blue eyes, whose bright orbs flashed lightning at their discharge, flew forth two pointed ogles; but, happily for our hero, hit only a vast piece of beef which he was then conveying into his plate, and harmless spent their force. The fair warrior perceived their miscarriage, and immediately from her fair bosom drew forth a deadly sigh. A sigh which none could have heard unmoved, and which was sufficient at once to have swept off a dozen beaus; so soft, so sweet, so tender, that the insinuating air must have found its subtle way to the heart of our hero, had it not luckily been driven from his ears by the coarse bubbling of some bottled ale, which at that time he was pouring forth. Many other weapons did she assay; but the god of eating (if there be any such deity, for I do not confidently assert it) preserved his votary; or perhaps it may not be *dignus vindice nodus*, and the present security of Jones may be accounted for by natural means; for as love frequently preserves from the attacks of hunger, so may hunger possibly, in some cases, defend us against love.

The fair one, enraged at her frequent disappointments, determined on a short cessation of arms. Which interval she employed in making ready every engine of amorous warfare for the renewing of the attack when dinner should be over.

No sooner then was the cloth removed than she again began her operations. First, having planted her right eye sidewise against Mr Jones, she shot from its corner a most penetrating glance; which, though great part of its force was spent before it reached our hero, did not vent itself absolutely without effect. This the fair one perceiving, hastily withdrew her eyes, and levelled them downwards, as if she was concerned for what she had done; though by this means she designed only to draw him from his guard, and indeed to open his eyes, through which she intended to surprise his heart. And now, gently lifting up those two bright orbs which had already begun to make an impression on poor Jones, she discharged a volley of small charms at once from her whole countenance in a smile. Not a smile of mirth, nor of joy; but a smile of affection, which most ladies have always ready at their command, and which serves them to show at once their good-humour, their pretty dimples, and their white teeth.

This smile our hero received full in his eyes, and was immediately staggered with its force. He then began to see the designs of the enemy, and indeed to feel their success. A parley now was set on foot between the parties; during which the artful fair so slyly and imperceptibly carried on her attack, that she had almost subdued the heart of our hero before she again repaired to acts of hostility. To confess the truth, I am afraid Mr Jones maintained a kind of Dutch defence, and treacherously delivered up the garrison, without duly weighing his allegiance to the fair Sophia. In short, no sooner had the amorous parley ended and the lady had unmasked the royal battery, by carelessly letting her handkerchief drop from her neck, than the heart of Mr Jones was entirely taken, and the fair conqueror enjoyed the usual fruits of her victory.

Here the Graces think proper to end their description, and here we think proper to end the chapter.

✕ The Diamond of the Kitchen

Jean Anthelme Brillat-Savarin (1755–1826) was arguably the first full-blown literary gastronome. He fled France during the Revolution, but returned under the Directorate to write his Physiologie de la goût *(1825), which he dedicated to his beautiful and accomplished cousin, Juliette Récamier (she of the sofa). Although he never married, he was as interested in love as he was in gastronomy, and especially fascinated by the aphrodisiac reputation of the truffle.*

Truffle. As soon as the word is spoken, it awakens lustful and erotic memories among the skirt-wearing sex and erotic and lustful memories among the beard-wearing sex. This honorable parallelism comes not only from the fact that this esteemed tuber is delicious, but also because it is still believed to bring about potency, the exercise of which brings sweet pleasure …

At the time I write, the glory of the truffle is at its apogee. Let no one ever confess that he dined where truffles were not. However good any entrée may be, it seems bad unless enriched by truffles. Who has not felt his mouth water when any allusion was made to *truffes à la provençale*?

A sauté of truffles is a dish the honours of which the mistress of the house reserves to herself; in fine, the truffle is the diamond of the kitchen.

I sought the reason of this preference; it seemed to me that many other substances had an equal right to the honour, and I became satisfied that the cause was that the truffle was supposed to excite the genesiac sense. This I am sure is the chief quality of its perfection, and the predilection and preference evinced for it, so powerful is our servitude to this tyrannical and capricious sense.

This discovery led me to seek to ascertain if the effect were real or imaginary … I first approached the ladies, on account of their keen perception and sense of tact, but … all the replies were ironical or evasive. Only one lady was frank with me …

'Monsieur,' she said to me, 'one day long ago when suppers were still the fashion, I supped at home *en trio* with my husband and a friend of his. Verseuil was a handsome fellow, not without wit, and a frequent visitor to my house, but he had never said anything to me to make me look on him in the light of a prospective lover, and if he occasionally paid me compliments, they were so discreet that only a fool could have taken offence at them. On the day in question he seemed destined to keep me company for the rest of the evening, for my husband had a business appointment and was due to leave us before long. The basis of our supper, which was a light meal, was a superb truffled fowl which the sub-delegate from Perigueux had sent us in those days when such a dish was a great luxury, and you can guess from its origin that in this case it was perfection itself. The truffles in particular were delicious, and you know how I love them. All the same, I restrained myself, and what is more, I drank only one glass of champagne; I had some sort of womanly premonition that something would happen before the evening was out. After a while my husband went off, leaving me alone with Verseuil, whom he regarded as perfectly harmless. At first we talked of matters of no consequence, but soon the conversation took a much narrower and more interesting turn. Verseuil was first complimentary, then expansive, affectionate, and tender, and finally, when he saw that I was simply amused by his sweet nothings, so importunate that I could no longer have any doubts about his intentions. At that point I awoke as from a dream, and defended myself all the more sincerely in that my heart said nothing to me in his favour. He persisted, with an ardour which seemed likely to become dangerous; I was hard put to keep him at arm's length, and I admit to my shame that I only succeeded in doing so by persuading him that all hope was not denied to him in the future. Finally, he took his leave, I went to bed and slept heavily. But the next day was the day of judgment; I examined my conduct of the previous evening and found it reprehensible … My pride ought to have been aroused earlier, and, my eyes armed with severity, I should have rung the bell, screamed, flown into a rage … What shall I say, Monsieur? I put it all down to the truffles.

Lucent Syrops, Tinct with Cinnamon

John Keats (1795–1826) describes the exquisite feast which Porphyro laid out to arouse Madeleine in his 1819 poem 'The Eve of St Agnes'. It was inspired by the superstition that if a girl went to bed naked on St Agnes Eve (20 January), she would see her future husband in a dream.

Then by the bed-side, where the faded moon
Made a dim, silver twilight, soft he set
A table, and, half anguish'd, threw thereon
A cloth of woven crimson, gold, and jet:
O for some drowsy Morphean amulet!
The boisterous, midnight, festive clarion,
The kettle-drum, and far-heard clarinet,
Affray his ears, though but in dying tone:
The hall door shuts again, and all the noise is gone.

And still she slept an azure-lidded sleep,
In blanched linen, smooth, and lavender'd,
While he from forth the closet brought a heap
Of candied apple, quince, and plum, and gourd;
With jellies soother than the creamy curd,
And lucent syrops, tinct with cinnamon;
Manna and dates, in argosy transferr'd
From Fez; and spiced dainties, every one,
From silken Samarcand to cedar'd Lebanon.

These delicates he heap'd with glowing hand
On golden dishes and in baskets bright
Of wreathed silver: sumptuous they stand
In the retired quiet of the night,
Filling the chilly room with perfume light.
'And now, my love, my seraph fair, awake!
Thou art my heaven, and I thine eremite:
Open thine eyes, for meek St Agnes' sake,

Or I shall drowse beside thee, so my soul doth ache.'
Thus whispering, his warm, unnerved arm
Sank in her pillow. Shaded was her dream
By the dusk curtains: 'twas a midnight charm
Impossible to melt as iced stream:
The lustrous salvers in the moonlight gleam;
Broad golden fringe upon the carpet lies:
It seem'd he never, never could redeem
From such a steadfast spell his lady's eyes;
So mus'd awhile, entoil'd in woofed phantasies.

Awakening up, he took her hollow lute,
Tumultuous, and, in chords that tenderest be,
He play'd an ancient ditty, long since mute,
In Provence call'd, 'La belle dame sans mercy':
Close to her ear touching the melody;
Wherewith disturb'd, she utter'd a soft moan:
He ceased – she panted quick – and suddenly
Her blue affrayed eyes wide open shone:
Upon his knees he sank, pale as smooth-sculptured stone.

✖ A Sybarite's Most Pamper'd Wishes

In Canto III of his Don Juan *(begun in 1819 and still unfinished when the poet died in 1824), Lord Byron describes the feast on an island in the Cyclades with which Haidée celebrates her passion for the shipwrecked Don Juan. It is seen through the eyes of an indignant witness, Haidée's long-lost pirate father Lambro.*

Old Lambro pass'd unseen a private gate,
And stood within his hall at eventide;
Meantime the lady and her lover sate
At wassail in their beauty and their pride:
An ivory inlaid table spread with state
Before them, and fair slaves on every side;
Gems, gold, and silver, form'd the service mostly,
Mother of pearl and coral the less costly.

The dinner made about a hundred dishes;
Lamb and pistachio nuts – in short, all meats,
And saffron soups, and sweetbreads; and the fishes
Were of the finest that e'er flounced in nets,
Drest to a Sybarite's most pamper'd wishes;
The beverage was various sherbets
Of raisin, orange, and pomegranate juice,
Squeezed through the rind, which makes it best for use.

These were ranged round, each in its crystal ewer,
And fruits, and date-bread loaves closed the repast,
And Mocha's berry, from Arabia pure,
In small fine China cups, came in at last;
Gold cups of filigree made to secure
The hand from burning underneath them placed,
Cloves, cinnamon, and saffron too were boil'd
Up with the coffee, which (I think) they spoil'd.

The hangings of the room were tapestry, made
Of velvet panels, each of different hue,
And thick with damask flowers of silk inlaid;
And round them ran a yellow border too;
The upper border, richly wrought, display'd,
Embroider'd delicately o'er with blue,
Soft Persian sentences, in lilac letters,
From poets, or the moralists their betters.

These Oriental writings on the wall,
Quite common in those countries, are a kind
Of monitors adapted to recall,
Like skulls at Memphian banquets, to the mind
The words which shook Belshazzar in his hall,
And took his kingdom from him: You will find,
Though sages may pour out their wisdom's treasure,
There is no sterner moralist than Pleasure.
A beauty at the season's close grown hectic,
A genius who has drunk himself to death,
A rake turn'd methodistic, or Eclectic
(For that's the name they like to pray beneath) –
But most, an alderman struck apoplectic,
Are things that really take away the breath, –
And show that late hours, wine, and love are able
To do not much less damage than the table.

Sirens of Spring

The poet and novelist Mortimer Collins (1827–1876) makes salad ingredients
into symbols of his own frustrated passion.

O cool in the summer is salad,
And warm in the winter is love;
And a poet shall sing you a ballad
Delicious thereon and thereof.
A singer am I, if no sinner,
My muse has a marvellous wing,
And I willingly worship at dinner
The sirens of Spring.

Take endive – like love it is bitter,
Take beet – for like love it is red;
Crisp leaf of the lettuce shall glitter,
And cress from the rivulet's bed,
Anchovies, foam-born, like the lady
Whose beauty has maddened this bard;
And olives, from groves that are shady;
And eggs – boil 'em hard.

✕ Too Much Fuss and Bustle

In this Moscow restaurant scene, Leo Tolstoy (1828–1910) subtly counterpoints Levin's idealistic hopes of marrying Kitty with the unfaithful Oblonsky's wordly interest in food (Anna Karenina, 1878).

When Levin went into the restaurant with Oblonsky, he could not help noticing a certain peculiarity of expression, as it were, a restrained radiance, about the face and whole figure of Stepan Arkadyevitch. Oblonsky took off his overcoat, and with his hat over one ear walked into the dining room, giving directions to the Tatar waiters, who were clustered about him in evening coats, bearing napkins. Bowing to right and left to the people he met, and here as everywhere joyously greeting acquaintances, he went up to the sideboard for a preliminary appetizer of fish and vodka, and said to the painted Frenchwoman decked in ribbons, lace, and ringlets, behind the counter, something so amusing that even that Frenchwoman was moved to genuine laughter. Levin for his part refrained from taking any vodka simply because he felt such a loathing of that Frenchwoman, all made up, it seemed, of false hair, *poudre de riz*, and *vinaigre de toilette*. He made haste to move away from her, as from a dirty place. His whole soul was filled with memories of Kitty, and there was a smile of triumph and happiness shining in his eyes …

'This way, your excellency, please. Your excellency won't be disturbed here,' said a particularly pertinacious, white-headed old Tatar with immense hips and coat-tails gaping widely behind. 'Walk in, your excellency,' he said to Levin; by way of showing his respect to Stepan Arkadyevitch, being attentive to his guest as well.

Instantly flinging a fresh cloth over the round table under the bronze chandelier, though it already had a table cloth on it, he pushed up velvet chairs, and came to a standstill before Stepan Arkadyevitch with a napkin and a bill of fare in his hands, awaiting his commands.

'If you prefer it, your excellency, a private room will be free directly; Prince Golitsin with a lady. Fresh oysters have come in.'

'Ah! oysters.'

Stepan Arkadyevitch became thoughtful.

'How if we were to change our program, Levin?' he said, keeping his finger on the bill of fare. And his face expressed serious hesitation. 'Are the oysters good? Mind now.'

'They're Flensburg, your excellency. We've no Ostend.'

'Flensburg will do, but are they fresh?'

'Only arrived yesterday.'

'Well, then, how if we were to begin with oysters, and so change the whole program? Eh?'

'It's all the same to me. I should like cabbage soup and porridge better than anything; but of course there's nothing like that here.'

'*Porridge à la Russe*, your honor would like?' said the Tatar, bending down to Levin, like a nurse speaking to a child.

'No, joking apart, whatever you choose is sure to be good. I've been skating, and I'm hungry. And don't imagine,' he added, detecting a look of dissatisfaction on Oblonsky's face, 'that I shan't appreciate your choice. I am fond of good things.'

'I should hope so! After all, it's one of the pleasures of life,' said Stepan Arkadyevitch. 'Well, then, my friend, you give us two − or better say three − dozen oysters, clear soup with vegetables ...'

'Printanière,' prompted the Tatar. But Stepan Arkadyevitch apparently did not care to allow him the satisfaction of giving the French names of the dishes.

'With vegetables in it, you know. Then turbot with thick sauce, then ... roast beef; and mind it's good. Yes, and capons, perhaps, and then sweets.'

The Tatar, recollecting that it was Stepan Arkadyevitch's way not to call the dishes by the names in the French bill of fare, did not repeat them after him, but could not resist rehearsing the whole menu to himself according to the bill: '*Soupe printanière, turbot, sauce Beaumarchais, poulard à l'estragon, macédoine de fruits* ... etc.,' and then instantly, as though worked by springs, laying down one bound bill of fare, he took up another, the list of wines, and submitted it to Stepan Arkadyevitch.

'What shall we drink?'

'What you like, only not too much. Champagne,' said Levin.

'What! to start with? You're right though, I dare say. Do you like the white seal?'

'*Cachet blanc,*' prompted the Tatar.

'Very well, then, give us that brand with the oysters, and then we'll see.'

'Yes, sir. And what table wine?'

'You can give us Nuits. Oh, no, better the classic Chablis.'

'Yes, sir. And *your* cheese, your excellency?'

'Oh, yes, Parmesan. Or would you like another?'

'No, it's all the same to me,' said Levin, unable to suppress a smile.

And the Tatar ran off with flying coat-tails, and in five minutes darted in with a dish of opened oysters on mother-of-pearl shells, and a bottle between his fingers.

Stepan Arkadyevitch crushed the starchy napkin, tucked it into his waistcoat, and settling his arms comfortably, started on the oysters.

'Not bad,' he said, stripping the oysters from the pearly shell with a silver fork, and swallowing them one after another. 'Not bad,' he repeated, turning his dewy, brilliant eyes from Levin to the Tatar.

Levin ate the oysters indeed, though white bread and cheese would have pleased him better. But he was admiring Oblonsky. Even the Tatar, uncorking the bottle and pouring the sparkling wine into the delicate glasses, glanced at Stepan Arkadyevitch, and settled his white cravat with a perceptible smile of satisfaction.

'You don't care much for oysters, do you?' said Stepan Arkadyevitch, emptying his wine glass, 'or you're worried about something. Eh?'

He wanted Levin to be in good spirits. But it was not that Levin was not in good spirits; he was ill at ease. With what he had in his soul, he felt sore and uncomfortable in the restaurant, in the midst of private rooms where men were dining with ladies, in all this fuss and bustle; the surroundings of bronzes, looking glasses, gas, and waiters – all of it was offensive to him. He was afraid of sullying what his soul was brimful of.

Wineskins of Brown Morbidity

DH Lawrence (1885–1930) wrote his sensuous poem 'Medlars and Sorb-Apples' while staying in San Gervasio, near Florence. It was published in his collection Birds, Beasts and Flowers *in 1923.*

I love you, rotten,
Delicious rottenness.

I love to suck you out from your skins
So brown and soft and coming suave,
So morbid, as the Italians say.

What a rare, powerful, reminiscent flavour
Comes out of your falling through the stages of decay:
Stream within stream.

Something of the same flavour as Syracusan muscat wine
Or vulgar Marsala.

Though even the word Marsala will smack of preciosity
Soon in the pussy-foot West.

What is it?
What is it, in the grape turning raisin,
In the medlar, in the sorb-apple.
Wineskins of brown morbidity,
Autumnal excrementa;
What is it that reminds us of white gods?

Gods nude as blanched nut-kernels.
Strangely, half-sinisterly flesh-fragrant
As if with sweat,
And drenched with mystery.

Sorb-apples, medlars with dead crowns.
I say, wonderful are the hellish experiences
Orphic, delicate
Dionysos of the Underworld.
A kiss, and a vivid spasm of farewell, a moment's orgasm
of rupture.
Then along the damp road alone, till the next turning.
And there, a new partner, a new parting, a new unfusing
into twain,
A new gasp of further isolation,
A new intoxication of loneliness, among decaying, frost-cold
leaves.

Plans for Domestic Delights

The poet Rainer Maria Rilke (1875–1926) wrote this letter to his future wife Clara Westhoff from Schmargendorf, near Berlin, on 23 October, 1900.

That evening, as we sat together in the little blue dining room, we also spoke of other things: In the cottage there would be light, a soft, veiled lamp, and I would stand at my stove and prepare a supper for you: a fine vegetable or cereal dish, and thick honey would gleam on a glass plate, and cold butter as pure as ivory would form a gentle contrast to the gaiety of a Russian table-cloth. Bread would have had to be there, strong, coarse-grained bread and rusks, and on a long narrow dish somewhat pale Westphalian ham, streaked with bands of white fat like an evening sky with long-drawn-out clouds.

Tea would stand ready for the drinking, gold-yellow tea in glasses with silver holders, exhaling a delicate fragrance, that fragrance which blended with the Hamburg rose and which would also blend with white carnations or fresh pineapple … Great lemons, cut in slices, would sink like suns into the golden dusk of the tea, dimly shining through it with the radiant flesh of their fruit, and its clear, glassy surface would tremble from the sour, rising juices. Red mandarins should be there, in which a summer is folded up very small like an Italian silk handkerchief in a nutshell. And roses would be about us, tall ones, nodding on their stems, and reclining ones, gently raising their heads, and the kind that wander from hand to hand, like girls in the figure of a dance.

So I dreamed. Premature dreams; the cottage is empty and cold, and my apartment here too is empty and cold: God knows how it is to become habitable. But even so I cannot believe that reality is not to achieve some relation to what I dreamed. I sent you yesterday a little package of a very excellent oat cereal to try. Directions on the package. Only it is good to let it cook somewhat longer than the fifteen minutes prescribed. Before eating put a piece of butter in it, or take apple sauce with it. I like best to eat it with butter, day in and day out. In fifteen minutes, the whole meal is ready, that is, boiling water must already have been made; it is put on hot then, and cooks

fifteen to twenty minutes. If you send for a patent 'all purpose' double boiler from a big household-goods store, you hardly need to stir it; the danger of burning is very slight then. Try it, give me a report. The big California firm has other glorious preparations also. I will send the catalogue shortly. For the rest, you know that I imagined an industrious day before that richly dreamed of supper. Isn't that so?

✗ Daisies of the Deep

Richard Le Gallienne (1866–1947) published his Little Dinners with the Sphinx and Other Prose Fancies *in 1896. The inspiration for the Sphinx was his then mistress, later wife, Julie Norregard. The couple separated in 1903 after six stormy years.*

The Sphinx and I were seated a few evenings ago at our usual little dinner, in our usual little sheltered corner, on the Lover's Gallery of one of the great London restaurants. The Sphinx says that there is only one place in Europe where one can really dine, but as it is impossible to be always within reasonable train service of that Montsalvat of cookery, she consents to eat with me – she cannot call it dine – at the restaurant of which I speak. I being very simple-minded, untravelled, and unlanguaged, think it, in my Cockney heart, a very fine place indeed, with its white marble pillars surrounding the spacious peristyle, and flashing with a thousand brilliant lights and colours; with its stately cooks, clothed in white samite, mystic, wonderful, ranged behind a great altar loaded with big silver dishes, and the sacred musicians of the temple ranged behind them – while in and out go the waiters, clothed in white and black, waiters so good and kind that I am compelled to think of Elijah being waited on by angels.

They have such an eye for a romance, too, and really take it personally to heart if it should befall that our little table is usurped by others that know not love. I like them, too, because they really seem to have an eye for the strange beauty and charm of the Sphinx, quite an unexpected taste for Botticelli. They ill conceal their envy of my lot, and sometimes, in the meditative pauses between the courses, I see them romantically reckoning how it might be possible by desperately saving up, by prodigious windfalls of tips, from unexampled despatch and sweetness in their ministrations, how it might be possible in ten years' time, perhaps even in five – the lady would wait five years! and her present lover could be artistically poisoned meanwhile! – how it might be possible to come and sue for her beautiful hand. Then a harsh British cry for 'waiter' comes like a rattle and scares away that beautiful dream-bird, though, as the poor dreamer speeds on the quest of

roast beef for four, you can see it still circling with its wonderful blue feathers around his pomatumed head.

Ah, yes, the waiters know that the Sphinx is no ordinary woman. She cannot conceal even from them the mystical star of her face, they too catch far echoes of the strange music of her brain, they too grow dreamy with dropped hints of fragrance from the rose of her wonderful heart.

How reverently do they help her doff her little cloak of silk and lace! with what a worshipful inclination of the head, as in the presence of a deity, do they await her verdict of choice between rival soups – shall it be 'clear or thick'? And when she decides on 'thick,' how relieved they seem to be, as if – well, some few matters remain undecided in the universe, but never mind, this is settled for ever – no more doubts possible on one portentous issue, at any rate – Madame will take her soup 'thick.'

'On such a night' our talk fell upon whitebait.

As the Sphinx's silver fork rustled among the withered silver upon her plate, she turned to me and said:

'Have you ever thought what beautiful little things these whitebait are?'

'Oh, yes,' I replied, 'they are the daisies of the deep sea, the three-penny-pieces of the ocean.'

'You dear!' said the Sphinx, who is alone in the world in thinking me awfully clever. 'Go on, say something else, something pretty about whitebait – there's a subject for you!'

✕ Venus in the Kitchen

The last book by the novelist and travel-writer Norman Douglas (1868–1952) was a delightful guide to aphrodisiac eating called Venus in the Kitchen or Love's Cookery Book *(1952), written under the nom de plume of Pilaff Bey. 'With its air of scholarship, its blend of the practical and the wildly impractical, the crispness of its comments, this book will be one of my favourite Douglas's' wrote his friend Graham Greene in his introduction to it. Douglas explains how he came to write it in his preface; a dish from it appears in the Literary Recipes section.*

I began one night twelve years ago after we had enjoyed a succulent dinner with several bottle of old red wine, followed by bitter lamentations on the part of the older members of the party over their declining vigour, in the course of which one of them remarked: 'Something might be done in the way of culinary recipes', adding that a well-known authority, Liebault, had written on the rejuvenating effects of certain condiments and certain dishes, I was then deputed, or rather implored, to look into the subject, and to note down such recipes as might apply to their case. This I did, supplying them with copies …

I kept the recipes in the bottom of my trunk, adding a fresh one every now and then, and also an occasional freak dish of an aphrodisiacal nature. There they would have stayed but for a member of the group of friends … He tried one or two of them and was favourably impressed by their subsequent effects. They Worked, he said. H begged me to have them printed, and said that in doing so I might confer a benefit on some poor devil. The poor devil must be a rich one, else he had better abandon all hope of encountering Venus, and retain that frigidity for which the economical recipes of ordinary cookery books are responsible. Well, I hope the poor devil, whoever he is, will follow his example and achieve the same happy results.

4 Childish Things

*Young children and chickens would
ever be eating.*

Thomas Tusser, *Five Hundred Points of Good Huswifery*

✕ A Call to Breakfast

The American poet Lydia Sigourney (1791–1865) was known as 'the sweet singer
of Hartford': poems like these saccharine-soaked lines were then much admired.

Breakfast! come to breakfast!
Little ones and all, –
How their merry footsteps
Patter at the call!
Break the bread; pour freely
Milk that cream-like flows;
A blessing on their appetites
And on their lips of rose.

Breakfast! summer breakfast!
Throw the casement high,
And catch the warblers' carol
On glad wing glancing by.
Set flowers upon your table
Impearled with dew-drops rare,
For still their fragrance speaks of Him
Who made this earth so fair.

Breakfast! winter breakfast!
Recruit the blazing fire;
Heap coal upon the glowing grate.
Or fill the furnace higher.
Though drifted snows descending –
May whiten field and bower,
Where loving hearts are true and warm,
King Frost hath little power.

✕ Lines from Ache-Inside

Probably more popular with children were the many skits on poems such as the previous one. Here the Victorian playwright Henry Sambrooke Leigh (1837–1883) parodies both the poems of Mark Akenside (whom Edward Gosse called 'a sort of frozen Keats') and Wordsworth with 'Only Seven (a pastoral story, after Wordsworth)'.

I marvelled why a simple child,
That lightly draws its breath,
Should utter groans so very wild,
And look as pale as death.

Adopting a parental tone,
I asked her why she cried;
The damsel answered with a groan,
'I've got a pain inside.

I thought it would have sent me mad,
Last night about eleven.'
Said I, 'What is it makes you bad?
How many apples have you had?'
She answered, 'Only seven!'

'And are you sure you took no more,
My little maid,' quoth I.
'Oh, please, sir, mother gave me four,
But they were in a pie.'

'If that's the case,' I stammered out,
'Of course you've had eleven.'
The maiden answered with a pout,
'I ain't had more nor seven!'

I wondered hugely what she meant,
And said, 'I'm bad at riddles,
But I know where little girls are sent
For telling tarradiddles.

Now if you don't reform,' said I,
'You'll never go to heaven!'
But all in vain; each time I try,
The little idiot makes reply,
'I ain't had more nor seven!'

PS
To borrow Wordsworth's name was wrong,
Or slightly misapplied;
And so I'd better call my song,
'Lines from Ache-inside.'

✕ Snapdragon

Children loved the ancient and dangerous Christmas game of Snapdragon, a finale to dinner which requires players to pluck flaming raisins out of a heaped dish, chanting this folk rhyme (Robert Chambers' Book of Days, *1864).*

Here he comes with flaming bowl,
Don't he mean to take his toll,
Snip! Snap! Dragon!
Take care you don't take too much,
Be not greedy in your clutch,
Snip! Snap! Dragon!
With his blue and lapping tongue
Many of you will be stung,
Snip! Snap! Dragon!
For he snaps at all that comes
Snatching at his feast of plums,
Snip! Snap! Dragon!
But Old Christmas makes him come,
Though he looks so fee! fa! fum!
Snip! Snap! Dragon!
Don't 'ee fear him but be bold —
Out he goes his flames are cold,
Snip! Snap! Dragon!

✗ The Flying Egg

Carlo Collodi (1826–1890) was a political satirist, and his famous children's story The Adventures of Pinocchio *(1883) poked fun at Italy's rulers as well as using anarchic nonsense to teach a tough, black-and-white morality to children. (Translated by Mary Alice Murray, 1914)*

Night was coming on and Pinocchio, remembering that he had eaten nothing all day, began to feel a gnawing in his stomach that very much resembled appetite.

After a few minutes his appetite had become hunger and in no time his hunger became ravenous.

Poor Pinocchio ran quickly to the fireplace, where a saucepan was boiling, and was going to take off the lid to see what was in it, but the saucepan was only painted on the wall. You can imagine his feelings. His nose, which was already long, became longer by at least three inches.

He then began to run about the room, searching in the drawers and in every imaginable place, in hopes of finding a bit of bread. If it was only a bit of dry bread, a crust, a bone left by a dog, a little mouldy pudding of Indian corn, a fish bone, a cherry stone—in fact, anything that he could gnaw. But he could find nothing, nothing at all, absolutely nothing.

And in the meanwhile his hunger grew and grew. Poor Pinocchio had no other relief than yawning, and his yawns were so tremendous that sometimes his mouth almost reached his ears. And after he had yawned he spluttered and felt as if he were going to faint.

Then he began to cry desperately, and he said:

'The Talking-Cricket was right. I did wrong to rebel against my papa and to run away from home. If my papa were here I should not now be dying of yawning! Oh! what a dreadful illness hunger is!'

Just then he thought he saw something in the dust-heap—something round and white that looked like a hen's egg. To give a spring and seize hold of it was the affair of a moment. It was indeed an egg.

Pinocchio's joy was beyond description. Almost believing it must be a dream he kept turning the egg over in his hands, feeling it and kissing it. And as he kissed it he said:

'And now, how shall I cook it? Shall I make an omelette? No, it would be better to cook it in a saucer! Or would it not be more savoury to fry it in the frying-pan? Or shall I simply boil it? No, the quickest way of all is to cook it in a saucer: I am in such a hurry to eat it!'

Without loss of time he placed an earthenware saucer on a brazier full of red-hot embers. Into the saucer instead of oil or butter he poured a little water; and when the water began to smoke, tac! he broke the egg-shell over it and let the contents drop in. But, instead of the white and the yolk a little chicken popped out very gay and polite. Making a beautiful courtesy it said to him:

'A thousand thanks, Master Pinocchio, for saving me the trouble of breaking the shell. Adieu until we meet again. Keep well, and my best compliments to all at home!'

Thus saying, it spread its wings, darted through the open window and, flying away, was lost to sight.

The poor puppet stood as if he had been bewitched, with his eyes fixed, his mouth open, and the egg-shell in his hand. Recovering, however, from his first stupefaction, he began to cry and scream, and to stamp his feet on the floor in desperation, and amidst his sobs he said:

'Ah, indeed, the Talking-Cricket was right. If I had not run away from home, and if my papa were here, I should not now be dying of hunger! Oh! what a dreadful illness hunger is!'

✗ Taste Them and Try

Christina Rossetti (1830–1894) dedicated her magical poem Goblin Market *(1862) to her sister: its colourful imagery and enticing description of forbidden fruits fascinates children, but it has a deeper meaning as an allegory of sexual temptation and renunciation.*

Morning and evening
Maids heard the goblins cry:
'Come buy our orchard fruits,
Come buy, come buy:
Apples and quinces,
Lemons and oranges,
Plump unpecked cherries,
Melons and raspberries,
Bloom-down-cheeked peaches,
Swart-headed mulberries,
Wild free-born cranberries,
Crab-apples, dewberries,
Pine-apples, blackberries,
Apricots, strawberries –
All ripe together
In summer weather –
Morns that pass by,
Fair eves that fly;
Come buy, come buy:
Our grapes fresh from the vine,
Pomegranates full and fine,
Dates and sharp bullaces,
Rare pears and greengages,
Damsons and bilberries,
Taste them and try:
Currant and gooseberries,
Bright-fire-like barberries,
Figs to fill your mouth,
Citrons from the South,

Sweet to tongue and sound to eye;
Come buy, come buy ...'

Sweet-tooth Laura spoke in haste:
'Good folk, I have no coin;
To take were to purloin:
I have no copper in my purse,
I have no silver either,
And all my gold is on the furze
That shakes in windy weather
Above the rusty heather.'
'You have much gold upon your head,'
They answer'd all together:
'Buy from us with a golden curl.'
She clipp'd a precious golden lock,
She dropp'd a tear more rare than pearl,
Then suck'd their fruit globes fair or red:
Sweeter than honey from the rock,
Stronger than man-rejoicing wine,
Clearer than water flow'd that juice;
She never tasted such before,
How should it cloy with length of use?
She suck'd and suck'd and suck'd the more
Fruits which that unknown orchard bore;
She suck'd until her lips were sore;
Then flung the emptied rinds away
But gather'd up one kernel stone,
And knew not was it night or day
As she turn'd home alone.

✕ Toasted Cheese and Milk

The Swiss novelist and children's author Johanna Spyri (1827–1901) put many memories of her own childhood in an Alpine village into her famous children's story Heidi *(1880). (Translated by Elizabeth Stork, 1915)*

The grandfather put the thick cover on the bed while Heidi watched him. After it was all done, she said: 'What a nice bed I have now, and what a splendid cover! I only wish the evening was here, that I might go to sleep in it.'

'I think we might eat something first,' said the grandfather. 'Don't you think so?'

Heidi had forgotten everything else in her interest for the bed; but when she was reminded of her dinner, she noticed how terribly hungry she really was. She had had only a piece of bread and a cup of thin coffee very early in the morning, before her long journey. Heidi said approvingly: 'I think we might, grandfather!'

'Let's go down then, if we agree,' said the old man, and followed close behind her. Going up to the fireplace, he pushed the big kettle aside and reached for a smaller one that was suspended on a chain. Then sitting down on a three-legged stool, he kindled a bright fire. When the kettle was boiling, the old man put a large piece of cheese on a long iron fork, and held it over the fire, turning it to and fro, till it was golden-brown on all sides. Heidi had watched him eagerly. Suddenly she ran to the cupboard. When her grandfather brought a pot and the toasted cheese to the table, he found it already nicely set with two plates and two knives and the bread in the middle. Heidi had seen the things in the cupboard and knew that they would be needed for the meal.

'I am glad to see that you can think for yourself,' said the grandfather, while he put the cheese on top of the bread, 'but something is missing yet.'

Heidi saw the steaming pot and ran back to the cupboard in all haste. A single little bowl was on the shelf. That did not perplex Heidi though, for she saw two glasses standing behind. With those three things she returned to the table.

'You certainly can help yourself! Where shall you sit, though?' asked the grandfather, who occupied the only chair himself, Heidi flew to the hearth, and bringing back the little stool, sat down on it.

'Now you have a seat, but it is much too low. In fact, you are too little to reach the table from my chair. Now you shall have something to eat at last!' and with that the grandfather filled the little bowl with milk. Putting it on his chair, he pushed it as near to the stool as was possible, and in that way Heidi had a table before her. He commanded her to eat the large piece of bread and the slice of golden cheese. He sat down himself on a corner of the table and started his own dinner. Heidi drank without stopping, for she felt exceedingly thirsty after her long journey. Taking a long breath, she put down her little bowl.

'How do you like the milk?' the grandfather asked her.

'I never tasted better,' answered Heidi.

'Then you shall have more,' and with that the grandfather filled the little bowl again.

✕ Breakfast on the *Plunderer* and Robber Tea

In his linked magical fantasies The Midnight Folk *(1927) and* The Box of Delights *(1935) John Masefield (1878–1967) showed how well he under-stood both what and how children love to eat. The books are recognisably set in Ledbury, where Masefield spent his childhood – not far from Pershore, home of that 'ripe blue plum'. During his quest in* The Midnight Folk *for the lost Harker treasure, Kay is treated to breakfast on the* Plunderer.

'But come, Master Kay,' the Captain said, 'breakfast is on the table. Step down the ladder with me to the cabin' ...

They had for breakfast all the things that Kay was fondest of: very hot, little, round loaves of new white bread baked in the embers of a wood-fire, very salt butter, a sardine with a lot of olive oil, some minced kidneys, a poached egg and frizzled bacon, a very fat sausage all bursting out of its skin, a home-made pork-pie, with cold jelly and yolk of egg beneath the crust, a bowl of strawberries and cream with sifted sugar, a bowl of raspberries and cream with blobs of sugar-candyish brown sugar that you could scrunch, some nice new mushrooms and chicken, part of a honeycomb with cream, a cup of coffee with crystals of white sugar candy for a change, a yellow plum, a greengage and then a ripe blue plum of Pershore to finish off with.

Beware the abridged editions of The Box of Delights, *which foolishly omit Masefield's wonderful description of the game of Robber Tea.*

Robber Tea was one of Kay's delights. It was a game only played on winter evenings, in the dark old study that had shelves full of old books, and old guns on the walls above the shelves.

At the beginning of the game, the window curtains were drawn, so as to make a darkness. Then, the fire was built up with wood and coal, so as to make a hot toasting fire. Then the table was pulled to one side of the room against the bookshelves, and some dark curtains were brought down and spread over the table and adjoining chairs, so as to make an inner cave. When the cave had been rigged, it was lit with some lanterns that had coloured glass slides. When all this was ready, a waterproof sheet was spread on the hearthrug with a supply of toasting forks, sausages, bread, butter, dripping and strawberry jam. Then, the robbers lay in the glow of the fire toasting bread and sausages, and afterwards eating them in the inner cave.

✕ Two Picnics with Ratty

Kenneth Grahame (1859–1932) began The Wind in the Willows *(1908) in the form of bedtime stories and letters written to amuse his small son Alasdair; it celebrates his own excursions on the Thames with such friends as Arthur Quiller-Couch, who was never happier than when afloat, and who inspired the character of Ratty.*

A LUNCHEON BASKET FOR THE MOLE

'Look here! If you've really nothing else on hand this morning, supposing we drop down the river together, and have a long day of it?'

The Mole waggled his toes from sheer happiness, spread his chest with a sigh of full contentment, and leaned back blissfully into the soft cushions. '*What* a day I'm having!' he said. 'Let us start at once!'

'Hold hard a minute, then!' said the Rat. He looped the painter through a ring in his landing-stage, climbed up into his hole above, and after a short interval reappeared staggering under a fat, wicker luncheon-basket.

'Shove that under your feet,' he observed to the Mole, as he passed it down into the boat. Then he untied the painter and took the sculls again.

'What's inside it?' asked the Mole, wriggling with curiosity.

'There's cold chicken inside it,' replied the Rat briefly; 'cold-tonguecoldhamcoldbeefpickledgherkinssaladfrenchrollscresssandwich espottedmeatgingerbeerlemonadesodawater—'

'O stop, stop,' cried the Mole in ecstasies: 'This is too much!'

'Do you really think so?' enquired the Rat seriously. 'It's only what I always take on these little excursions; and the other animals are always telling me that I'm a mean beast and cut it *very* fine!'

A HAMPER FOR THE SEA RAT

'That reminds me,' said the polite Water Rat; 'you happened to mention that you were hungry, and I ought to have spoken earlier. Of course, you will stop and take your midday meal with me? My hole is close by; it is some time past noon, and you are very welcome to whatever there is.'

'Now I call that kind and brotherly of you,' said the Sea Rat. 'I was indeed hungry when I sat down, and ever since I inadvertently happened to mention shell-fish, my pangs have been extreme. But couldn't you fetch it along out here? I am none too fond of going under hatches, unless I'm obliged to; and then, while we eat, I could tell you more concerning my voyages and the pleasant life I lead— at least, it is very pleasant to me, and by your attention I judge it commends itself to you; whereas if we go indoors it is a hundred to one that I shall presently fall asleep.'

'That is indeed an excellent suggestion,' said the Water Rat, and hurried off home. There he got out the luncheon-basket and packed a simple meal, in which, remembering the stranger's origin and prefer-ences, he took care to include a yard of long French bread, a sausage out of which the garlic sang, some cheese which lay down and cried, and a long-necked straw-covered flask wherein lay bottled sunshine shed and garnered on far Southern slopes. Thus laden, he returned with all speed, and blushed for pleasure at the old seaman's commen-dations of his taste and judgment, as together they unpacked the basket and laid out the contents on the grass by the roadside.

✕ The Island Camp

Arthur Ransome (1884–1967) wrote Swallows and Amazons, *a book steeped in memories of his own childhood and first loves, in 1929, after he had settled down in the Lake Country following a ten-year exile in Russia and the Baltic. He had picnicked on Peel Island as a child and camped there as a young man; now he immortalised it as 'Wild Cat Island', temporary home of the enterprising Walker children.*

The camp now began to look really like a camp. There were the two tents slung between the two pairs of trees. The mate and the able-seaman were to sleep in one, and the captain and the boy in the other. Then in the open space under the trees the fire was burning merrily. The kettle had boiled, and was standing steaming on the ground. Susan was melting a big pat of butter in the frying-pan. In a pudding-basin beside her she had six raw eggs. She had cracked the eggs on the edge of a mug and broken them into the basin. Their empty shells were crackling in the fire. Four mugs stood in a row on the ground.

'No plates to-day,' said Mate Susan. 'We all eat out of the common dish.'

'But it isn't a common dish,' said Roger. 'It's a frying-pan.'

'Well, we eat out of it anyway. Egg's awful stuff for sticking to plates.'

She had now emptied the raw eggs into the sizzling butter, and was stirring the eggs and the butter together after shaking the pepper pot over them, and putting in a lot of salt.

'They're beginning to curdle,' said Titty, who was watching carefully. 'When they begin to flake, you have to keep scraping them off the bottom of the pan. I saw Mrs Jackson do it.'

'They're flaking now,' said Susan. 'Come on and scrape away.'

She put the frying-pan on the ground, and gave every one a spoon. The captain, mate, and the crew of *Swallow* squatted round the frying-pan, and began eating as soon as the scrambled eggs, which were very hot, would let them. Mate Susan had already cut four huge slices of brown bread and butter to eat with the eggs. Then she poured out four mugs of tea, and filled them up with milk from a bottle. 'There'll be enough milk in the bottle for to-day,' Mother had said, 'but for to-morrow we must try to find you milk from a farm a little nearer than Holly Howe.' Then there was a big rice pudding, which had been brought with them on the top of the things in one of the big biscuit tins. It too became a common dish, like the frying-pan. Then there were four big slabs of seed cake. Then there were apples all round.

✕ Turkish Delight

CS Lewis (1898–1963) made food a recurrent theme in Narnia, but never more vividly than in Edmund's seduction by sweetmeats in The Lion, the Witch and the Wardrobe *(1950).*

'It is dull, Son of Adam, to drink without eating,' said the Queen presently. 'What would you like best to eat?'

'Turkish Delight, please, your Majesty,' said Edmund.

The Queen let another drop fall from her bottle on to the snow, and instantly there appeared a round box, tied with green silk ribbon, which, when opened, turned out to contain several pounds of the best Turkish Delight. Each piece was sweet and light to the very centre and Edmund had never tasted anything more delicious. He was quite warm now, and very comfortable.

While he was eating the Queen kept asking him questions. At first Edmund tried to remember that it is rude to speak with one's mouth full, but soon he forgot about this and thought only of trying to shovel down as much Turkish Delight as he could, and the more he ate the more he wanted to eat, and he never asked himself why the Queen should be so inquisitive. She got him to tell her that he had one brother and two sisters, and that one of his sisters had already been in Narnia and had met a Faun there, and that no one except himself and his brother and his sisters knew anything about Narnia. She seemed especially interested in the fact that there were four of them, and kept on coming back to it. 'You are sure there are just four of you?' she asked. 'Two Sons of Adam and two Daughters of Eve, neither more nor less?' and Edmund, with his mouth full of Turkish Delight, kept on saying, 'Yes, I told you that before,' and forgetting to call her 'Your Majesty' but she didn't seem to mind now.

At last the Turkish Delight was all finished and Edmund was looking very hard at the empty box and wishing that she would ask him whether he would like some more. Probably the Queen knew quite well what he was thinking; for she knew, though Edmund did not, that this was enchanted Turkish Delight and that anyone who had once tasted it would want more and more of it, and would even, if they

were allowed, go on eating it till they killed themselves. But she did
not offer him any more. Instead, she said to him,

'Son of Adam, I should so much like to see your brother and your
two sisters. Will you bring them to me?'

'I'll try,' said Edmund, still looking at the empty box.

'Because, if you did come again – bringing them with you of course
– I'd be able to give you some more Turkish Delight. I can't do it now,
the magic will only work once. In my own house it would be another
matter.'

'Why can't we go to your house now?' said Edmund. When he had
first got on to the sledge he had been afraid that she might drive away
with him to some unknown place from which he would not be able
to get back, but he had forgotten about that fear now.

'It is a lovely place, my house,' said the Queen. 'I am sure you would
like it. There are whole rooms full of Turkish Delight, and what's more,
I have no children of my own. I want a nice boy whom I could bring
up as a Prince and who would be King of Narnia when I am gone.
While he was Prince he would wear a gold crown and eat Turkish
Delight all day long; and you are much the cleverest and handsomest
young man I've ever met. I think I would like to make you the Prince
– some day, when you bring the others to visit me.'

'Why not now?' said Edmund. His face had become very red and
his mouth and fingers were sticky. He did not look either clever or
handsome, whatever the Queen might say.

✕ Food Tastes So Much Nicer Out of Doors

Enid Blyton (1897–1968) stuffed her books with enjoyable feasts, preferably eaten outside. In Five on Kirrin Island Again *(1947) she jokingly acknowledges her famous cliché.*

'Anyone for a snack?' asked Dick, hopefully. But for once the children were too tired to sit through a proper meal so they munched on biscuits and some juicy plums, which Anne had packed at the last minute, finishing up with a bar of chocolate Julian found in his pocket.

'That was nice,' he said, licking the last crumb of chocolate from his fingers. But no one answered. They were all fast asleep.

George awoke to find Timmy licking her.

'Stop it, Tim, you've made my face all wet!' said George, pushing him away.

'He's giving you your morning bath,' grinned Dick, sitting up. 'Ooh, do I smell sausages being roasted?'

Anne was indeed roasting sausages on a campfire. The efficient little girl had woken up early, gathered firewood and set about preparing breakfast. She knew everyone would wake up ravenous.

'Quite the perfect little housewife,' said Julian as he speared a sausage on a stick and held it to the flames.

Anne smiled to herself. Her brothers often teased her about 'playing houses' but she knew that a lot of their adventures wouldn't have turned out so well if she hadn't taken care of the basics. Like food.

'Let's see what else we have,' said Dick, polishing off his third sausage and rummaging through the bag.

'Tongue, sardines, fresh tomatoes, a tin of pineapple chunks …'

'… and lashings of ginger beer' said George, fishing out four bottles from the depths of the now rather empty bag.

The children cut out chunks of tongue with a clean pocket knife that Julian always carried in his pocket. Anne had even remembered to pack some bread and butter, so they made huge, thick sandwiches, and ate them with the juicy tomatoes.

'This is so much fun,' said Anne. 'I always think …'

'… food tastes so much nicer eaten out of doors,' chimed in the rest, grinning at Anne's astonished face.

5 Cooks and Kitchens

*Through all the world there goes one long cry
from the heart of the artist: Give me leave to
do my utmost!*

Isak Dinesen, 'Babette's Feast', 1953

*Happiness: a good bank account, a good cook,
and a good digestion.*

Jean-Jacques Rousseau

On Thyself Thy Genius Must Depend

Supposedly written by Athenaeus of Naucratis (once a city on the Nile) sometime before AD 300, the Deipnosophistae *or Dinner-Table Philosophers is a cornucopia of information on the social customs of the times, with a special emphasis on dining — including this optimistic account of the perfect cook. This versified translation is from Isaac D'Israeli's* Curiosities of Literature *(1835).*

Know then, the Cook, a dinner that's bespoke
Aspiring to prepare, with prescient zeal
Should know the tastes and humours of the guests;
For if he drudges through the common work,
Thoughtless of manner, careless what the place
And seasons claim, and what the favouring hour
Auspicious to his genius may present,
Why, standing midst the multitude of men,
Call we this plodding fricasseer a COOK?
Oh differing far! and one is not the other!
We call indeed the general of an army
Him who is charged to lead it to the war;
But the true general is the man whose mind,
Mastering events, anticipates, combines;
Else is he but a leader to his men!
With our profession thus: the first who comes
May with a humble toil, or slice, or chop,
Prepare the ingredients, and around the fire
Obsequious, him I call a fricasseer!
But ah! the cook a brighter glory crowns!
Well skill'd is he to know the place, the hour,
Him who invites, and him who is invited,
What fish in season makes the market rich …
Look not in books for what some idle sage
So idly raved; for cookery is an art
Comporting ill with rhetoric; 'tis an art
Still changing, and of momentary triumph!

Know on thyself thy genius must depend.
All books of cookery, all helps of art,
All critic learning, all commenting notes,
Are vain, if void of genius, thou wouldst cook!'
The culinary sage thus spoke; his friend
Demands, 'Where is the ideal cook thou paint'st?'
'Lo, I the man!' the savouring sage replied.
'Now be thine eyes the witness of my art!
This tunny drest, so odorous shall steam,
The spicy sweetness so shall steal thy sense,
That thou in a delicious reverie
Shalt slumber heavenly o'er the Attic dish!' ...

I like to see the faces of my guests,
To feed them as their age and station claim.
My kitchen changes, as my guests inspire
The various spectacle; for lovers now,
Philosophers, and now for financiers.
If my young royster be a mettled spark,
Who melts an acre in a savoury dish
To charm his mistress, scuttle-fish and crabs,
And all the shelly race, with mixture due
Of cordials filtered, exquisitely rich.
For such a host, my friend! expends much more
In oil than cotton; solely studying love!
To a philosopher, that animal
Voracious, solid ham and bulky feet;
But to the financier, with costly niceness,
Glociscus rare, or rarity more rare.
Insensible the palate of old age,
More difficult than the soft lips of youth
To move, I put much mustard in their dish;
With quickening sauces make their stupor keen,
And lash the lazy blood that creeps within.

The Master Cook

Ben Jonson (1572–1637) wrote his masque Neptune's Triumph for the Return of Albion *for the Twelfth Night celebrations on 6 January, 1624; the sets were designed by Inigo Jones. Jonson and Jones are characterised as Poet and Cook in the opening scene of the masque, which likens Jones' masque designs to a cook's creations. Sadly, competition for places at the masque was so intense that James I cancelled the performance.*

Poet: You are not his majesty's confectioner, are you?
Cook: No, but one that has as good title to the room,
   his master-cook! … why he is the man of men
For a professor, he designs, he draws.
He paints, he carves, he builds, he fortifies;
Makes citadels of curious fowl and fish.
Some he dry-ditches, some moats round with broths,
Mounts marrow-bones, cuts fifty-angled custards,
Rears bulwark pies, and for his outerworks
He raiseth ramparts of immortal crust;
And teacheth all the tactics at one dinner:
What ranks, what files to put his dishes in;
The whole art military. Then he knows
The influence of the stars upon his meats,
And all their seasons, tempers, qualities;
And so to fit his relishes and sauces,
He has Nature in a pot, 'bove all the chemists,
Or bare-breech'd brethren of the rosy-cross.
He is an architect, an engineer,
A soldier, a physician, a philosopher,
A general mathematician!

✕ The Choice of a Cook

In his Gastronomy, or The Bon-Vivant's Guide *(1801) Joseph Berchoux
(1760–1838) emphasises the need to give a good cook his head, and to provide
him with the most modern appliances in his kitchen. Poor Hannah Glasse is
given another dressing-down.*

When forming your household, apply your chief care
To the choice of a COOK, of accomplishments rare.
That point's most important; – on him it depends
Your table to crowd with agreeable friends.
This artist alone can establish your fame,
By the pleasing reflections attach'd to your name.
With preference mark him, who, proud of his station,
Conceives himself born for the good of the nation;
In the kitchen, with dignity lays down the law,
Uncontrolled, in his sphere, as a Turkish Bashaw.
As glory he courts, when his aid you implore,
You may hold this discourse, to incite him the more. –

'Your fame, my good friend, has engaged my esteem;
'Be chief of my kitchen; – there govern supreme.
'Become, from this day, my sole umpire, my guide;
'O'er my pleasantest want, let your science preside.
'Like a despot, command; – cut and carve as you will.
'May my excellent dinners, prepared by your skill,
'Fix my volatile friends; by their senses deceived,
'Till my wit seem a sauce of the pleasure received!'
It is this, in your service, his zeal you excite;
And, when pleasure and duty together unite,
Most happy effects in all arts we command,
The proof is approaching; your guests are at hand.

Observe, in each face, how completely declared
Is a wish to partake of the banquet prepared!
Their eagerness chides the slow kitchen's delay;

Yet there, all's in motion; the stoves now display
Flames vivid and bright, whilst, above and around,
Thick vapours with savoury odours abound.
Here and there run the kitchen-maids, hurried and hot,
Now watching the stoves, now the spit or the pot;
But the Cook remains cool, his arrangements all made,
Well convinced the delay will be amply repaid …
'Mongst the implements used by the artist I sing,
To our minds, some the science of Chemistry bring;
While others, suspended in order exact,
Seem, in well polish'd metal, an army compact.
No iron tubes, here, vomit death from afar;
No brazen-mouth'd trumpets loud clamour for war;
But steel, copper and brass, our first want to supply,
All the flames that are raised by the bellows defy.
Place'd above, near the chimney, a complex machine,
Form'd of numerous wheels, slow revolving is seen;
Below, the meats roasting its impulse obeys,
Which chains, to the axis they turn on, convey,
With a sound that to Handel might grating appear,
But, the appetite courting, it pleases my ear …

I will not, for show, a long list introduce
Of the numerous dishes, which now are in use.
My muse, with a conduct reserved and discreet,
On so fertile a subject will sparingly treat;
The true sons of taste only anxious to please,
She disdains on so homely a topic to seize.
In *Glasse upon Cook'ry*, the vulgar may find
Receipts, which will probably prove to their mind;
With each country-bred cook, in mock-turtle may vie,
Or expect our applause when they've raised a pork-pie.

A Cook to the Centre of Her Soul

Harriet Beecher Stowe (1811–1896) was an authority on home-making: her magazine Hearth and Home *and her books on domestic matters earned her fame long before she wrote* Uncle Tom's Cabin *(1852), the tract for her times that lit the tinder under the Civil War. Its fourth chapter describes Uncle Tom's wife, Aunt Chloe.*

The cabin of Uncle Tom was a small log building, close adjoining to 'the house', as the negro *par excellence* designates his master's dwelling. In front it had a neat garden-patch, where, every summer, strawberries, raspberries, and a variety of fruits and vegetables, flourished under careful tending. The whole front of it was covered by a large scarlet bignonia and a native multiflora rose, which, entwisting and interlacing, left scarce a vestige of the rough logs to be seen. Here, also, in summer, various brilliant annuals, such as marigolds, petunias, four-o'clocks, found an indulgent corner in which to unfold their splendors, and were the delight and pride of Aunt Chloe's heart.

Let us enter the dwelling. The evening meal at the house is over, and Aunt Chloe, who presided over its preparation as head cook, has left to inferior officers in the kitchen the business of clearing away and washing dishes, and come out into her own snug territories, to 'get her ole man's supper'; therefore, doubt not that it is her you see by the fire, presiding with anxious interest over certain frizzling items in a stew-pan, and anon with grave consideration lifting the cover of a bake-kettle, from whence steam forth indubitable intimations of 'something good.' ... Her whole plump countenance beams with satisfaction and contentment from under her well-starched checked turban, bearing on it, however, if we must confess it, a little of that tinge of self-consciousness which becomes the first cook of the neighbourhood, as Aunt Chloe was universally held and acknowledged to be.

A cook she certainly was, in the very bone and centre of her soul. Not a chicken or turkey or duck in the barn-yard but looked grave when they saw her approaching, and seemed evidently to be reflecting on their latter end; and certain it was that she was always meditating on trussing, stuffing and roasting, to a degree that was calculated to inspire terror in any reflecting fowl living. Her corn-cake, in all its varieties of hoe-cake, dodgers, muffins, and other species too numerous to mention, was a sublime mystery to all less practised compounders; and she would shake her fat sides with honest pride and merriment, as she would narrate the fruitless efforts that one and another of her compeers had made to attain to her elevation.

The arrival of company at the house, the arranging of dinners and suppers 'in style,' awoke all the energies of her soul; and no sight was more welcome to her than a pile of travelling trunks launched on the veranda, for then she foresaw fresh efforts and fresh triumphs.

✖ Professors of Cookery?

*The great Victorian cook and cookery writer Alexis Soyer (1810–1858) pref-
aced his* A Shilling Cookery for the People *(1855), a cookbook which he
wrote to improve the diet of the masses, with a scientifically based plea for a
re-evaluation of the importance of the cook.*

Cookery, in our era, has been thought beneath the attention of men
of science; and yet, was there ever a political, commercial, or even a
domestic event, but what always has been, and always will be, celebrated either by a banquet or a dinner? And pray, who is answerable
for the comfort and conviviality of the guests of such festivals but
the cook, who has been intrusted with such important duties? The
selection of good and proper beverages will, of course, greatly assist
the cook's endeavours; but these may be purchased months, or even
years, before you require them, which would of course give you an
ample chance of remedying any error; while a dinner is the creation
of a day and the success of a moment. Therefore you will perceive
that nothing more disposes the heart to amicable feeling and friendly
transactions, than a dinner well conceived and artistically prepared. In
ancient times, a cook, especially if a man, was looked upon as a distinguished member of society; while now he is, in the opinion of almost
every one, a mere menial. Still there are a few who highly appreciate
the knowledge he possesses, especially in the higher circles, who have
classified cookery as a high art. For example, let us see what one of the
greatest chemists of the day (Liebig) says on this imperishable subject,
in his valuable work, *The Chemistry of Food*, that

> Among all the arts known to man there is none which enjoys a
> juster appreciation, and the products of which are more universally
> admired, than that which is concerned in the preparation of our
> food. Led by an instinct, which has almost reached the dignity of
> conscious knowledge, as the unerring guide, and by the sense of
> taste, which protects the health, the experienced cook, with respect
> to the choice, the admixture, and the preparation of food, has made
> acquisitions surpassing all that chemical and physiological science

SOYER'S MODERN HOUSEWIFE'S KITCHEN APPARATUS.
Containing an Open Roasting Fire, a Hot Water Boiler, a Baking Oven, a Broiling Stove,
a Hot Plate, &c., all heated by one Fire.
Height 2ft. 4in., Width 2ft., Length 3ft.

have done in regard to the doctrine or theory of nutrition. In soup and meat sauces, he imitates the gastric juice; and by the cheese which closes the banquet, he assists the action of the dissolved epithelium of the stomach. The table, supplied with dishes, appears to the observer like a machine, the parts of which are harmoniously fitted together, and so arranged that, when brought into action, a maximum of effect may be obtained by means of them. The able culinary artist accompanies the sanguineous matter with those which promote the process of solution and sanguification, in due proportion; he avoids all kinds of unnecessary stimuli, such as do not act in restoring the equilibrium; and he provides the due nourishment for the child or the weak old man, as well as for the strong of both sexes.

Such is the high eulogium paid to culinary science by that learned man; and perhaps there is no one more able of appreciating its value than him. Therefore I do not yet despair of seeing the day when that science, like others, will have its qualified professors.

✗ Energy and Bustle Personified

Alexandre Dumas (1802–1870) enjoyed cooking as much as he enjoyed writing novels. Frank Schloesser paints a vivid word portrait of him in The Greedy Book *(1906).*

In the kitchen, as in the theatre, the great novelist was master of all difficulties. He delighted to make a triumph of an opportunity of which others would only have made a failure. For himself he would have been content with a couple of eggs; but if, as he wrote, he heard the cook complaining, 'What shall I do? There are twenty to dinner this evening, and I have only three tomatoes left for my sauce! It is impossible!', then the master would lift his head and cry, 'Let me see what I can do!'. So saying, he would rush headlong into the kitchen just as he was in his usual working dress, with his shirt-sleeves rolled up above his elbows, and calling everybody in the place round him to watch his prowess, he would labour among the stewpans for a good hour, ordering all those who had followed him to the kitchen to different menial tasks: one to slice the carrots, one to peel potatoes, one to chop up herbs, turning them all into scullions in fact.

The blustering, boisterous genius as easily dominated the kitchen as he did the literary world of the time. His cooking was energy and bustle personified. Meat and butter were mingled with fine wines in the sauce-pans, half a dozen sauces were being watched in the bain-marie, and all the while he was cracking jokes and laughing at them most loudly himself. It was a wonderful and inspiring sight, and, as may be imagined, Dumas seasoned the conversation as well as the dishes with the spice of his wit and humour. No matter how serious his thoughts had been a few moments before, it seemed as if the atmosphere of the kitchen had the power to dissipate them. He forgot all his ever-present cares, and was radiant with grease and hilarity.

Then suddenly, without the slightest warning, he would utter a melodramatic scream and rush out of the kitchen to his study. He had remembered the final dénouement of a scene he had left unfinished. He would reinstate himself at his writing-table and take up the thread of the story as if no interruption whatever had occurred.

✕ A Perfect Model of Gastronomy

Since Alexandre Dumas was a gourmet of some pretensions, it is not surprising that food features large in his novels, and the food-loving Porthos is undoubtedly his alter ego. In The Vicomte de Bragelonne, or Ten Years Later *(1850), the third of his Three Musketeers novels, Porthos, now Baron de Valon, impresses Louis XIV with his appetite and culinary knowledge – with a little help on court etiquette from D'Artagnan. (Translated by HL Williams, 1893)*

Louis XIV was a formidable table-companion; he delighted to criticise his cooks; but when he honoured them by praise and commendation, the honour was overwhelming. The king began by eating several kinds of soup, either mixed together or taken separately. He intermixed, or rather he separated, each of the soups by a glass of old wine. He ate quickly and somewhat greedily. Porthos, who from the beginning had, out of respect, been waiting for a jog of D'Artagnan's arm, seeing the king make such rapid progress, turned to the musketeer and said in a low tone:

'It seems as if one might go on now; his majesty is very encouraging, from the example he sets. Look.'

'The king eats,' said D'Artagnan, 'but he talks at the same time; try and manage matters in such manner that, if he should happen to address a remark to you, he should not find you with your mouth full, which would be very disrespectful.'

'The best way in that case,' said Porthos, 'is to eat no supper at all; and yet I am very hungry, I admit, and everything looks and smells most invitingly, as if appealing to all my senses at once.'

'Don't think of not eating for a moment,' said D'Artagnan; 'that would put his majesty out terribly. The king has a saying, "that he who works well, eats well," and he does not like people to eat indifferently at his table.'

'How can I avoid having my mouth full if I eat?' said Porthos.

'All you have to do,' replied the captain of the musketeers, 'is simply to swallow what you have in it whenever the king does you the honour to address a remark to you.'

'Very good,' said Porthos: and from that moment he began to eat with a well-bred enthusiasm of manner.

The king occasionally looked at the different persons who were at table with him, and *en connoisseur*, could appreciate the different dispositions of his guests.

'Monsieur de Valon!' he said.

Porthos was enjoying a *salmi de lièvre*, and swallowed half of the back. His name pronounced in such a manner had made him start, and by a vigorous effort of his gullet he absorbed the whole mouthful.

'Sire,' replied Porthos, in a stifled voice, but sufficiently intelligible, nevertheless.

'Let those filets d'agneau be handed to Monsieur de Valon,' said the king. 'Do you like brown meats, M. de Valon?'

'Sire, I like everything,' replied Porthos.

D'Artagnan whispered, 'Everything your majesty sends me.'

Porthos repeated, 'Everything your majesty sends me,' an observation which the king apparently received with great satisfaction.

'People eat well who work well,' replied the king, delighted to have a guest who could eat as Porthos did. Porthos received the dish of lamb, and put a portion of it on his own plate.

'Well?' said the king.

'Exquisite,' said Porthos, calmly.

'Have you as good mutton in your part of the country, Monsieur de Valon?' continued the king.

'Sire, I believe that from my own province, as everywhere else, the best of everything is sent to Paris for your majesty's use; but, on the other hand, I do not eat lamb in the same way your majesty does.'

'Ah, ah! and how do you eat it?'

'Generally, I have a lamb dressed quite whole.'

'Quite whole?'

'Yes, sire.'

'In what manner, then?'

'In this, sire: My cook, who is a German, first stuffs the lamb in question with small sausages which he procures from Strasburg, force-meat balls which he procures from Troyes, and larks which he procures from Pithiviers: by some means or other, which I am not acquainted with, he bones the lamb as he would do a fowl, leaving the skin on, however, which forms a brown crust all over the animal; when it is cut in beautiful slices, in the same way as an enormous sausage, a rose-colored gravy pours forth, which is as agreeable to the eye as it is exquisite to the palate.' And Porthos finished by smacking his lips.

The king opened his eyes with delight, and, while cutting some of the *faisan en daube*, which was being handed to him, he said:

'That is a dish I should very much like to taste, Monsieur de Valon. Is it possible! a whole lamb!'

'Completely so, sire.'

'Pass those pheasants to M. de Valon; I perceive he is an amateur.'

The order was immediately obeyed. Then, continuing the conversation, he said: 'And you do not find the lamb too fat?'

'No, sire; the fat falls down at the same time as the gravy does, and swims on the surface: then the servant who carves removes the fat with a spoon, which I have had expressly made for that purpose.'

'Where do you reside?' inquired the king.

'At Pierrefonds, sire.'

'At Pierrefonds; where is that, M. de Valon – near Belle-Isle?'

'Oh, no, sire; Pierrefonds is in the Soissonnais.'

'I thought you alluded to the lamb on account of the salt marshes.'

'No, sire; I have marshes which are not salt, it is true, but which are not the less valuable on that account.'

The king had now arrived at the entremets, but without losing sight of Porthos, who continued to play his part in the best manner.

'You have an excellent appetite, M. de Valon,' said the king, 'and you make an admirable guest at table.'

'Ah, sire, if your majesty were ever to pay a visit to Pierrefonds, we would both of us eat our lamb together; for your appetite is not an indifferent one, by any means.'

D'Artagnan gave Porthos a severe kick under the table, which made Porthos colour up.

'At your majesty's present happy age,' said Porthos, in order to repair the mistake he had made, 'I was in the musketeers, and nothing could ever satisfy me then. Your majesty has an excellent appetite, as I have already had the honour of mentioning, but you select what you eat with too much refinement to be called a great eater.'

The king seemed charmed at his guest's politeness.

'Will you try some of these creams?' he said to Porthos.

'Sire, your majesty treats me with far too much kindness to prevent me speaking the whole truth.'

'Pray do so, M. de Valon.'

'Well, sire, with regard to sweet dishes. I only recognize pastry, and even that should be rather solid: all these frothy substances swell the stomach, and occupy a space which seems to me to be too precious to be so badly tenanted.'

'Ah! gentlemen,' said the king, indicating Porthos by a gesture, 'here is indeed a perfect model of gastronomy. It was in such a manner that our fathers, who so well knew what good living was, used to eat; while we,' added his majesty, 'can do nothing but trifle with our food.' And as he spoke he took the breast of a chicken, with ham, while Porthos attacked a dish of partridges and land-rails. The cup-bearer filled his majesty's glass. 'Give M. de Valon some of my wine,' said the king. This was one of the greatest honours of the royal table. D'Artagnan pressed his friend's knee.

'If you could only manage to swallow the half of that boar's head I see yonder,' said he to Porthos, 'I shall believe you will be a duke and peer within the next twelvemonth.'

'Presently,' said Porthos, phlegmatically; 'I shall come to it by-and-by.'

✕ The House Spun to Her Clamour

The Sahiba, or woman from Kulu, in Rudyard Kipling's Kim *(1901) was not only a wonderful cook, but also a mistress of healing.*

'I am old. I have borne sons in the body. Oh, once I could please men! Now I can cure them.' He heard her armlets tinkle as though she bared arms for action. 'I will take over the boy and dose him, and stuff him, and make him all whole. Hat! hai! We old people know something yet.'

Wherefore when Kim, aching in every bone, opened his eyes, and would go to the cook-house to get his master's food, he found strong coercion about him, and a veiled old figure at the door, flanked by the grizzled manservant, who told him very precisely the things that he was on no account to do.

'Thou must have? Thou shalt have nothing. What? A locked box in which to keep holy books? Oh, that is another matter. Heavens forbid I should come between a priest and his prayers! It shall be brought, and thou shalt keep the key.'

They pushed the coffer under his cot, and Kim shut away Mahbub's pistol, the oilskin packet of letters, and the locked books and diaries, with a groan of relief. For some absurd reason their weight on his shoulders was nothing to their weight on his poor mind. His neck ached under it of nights.

'Thine is a sickness uncommon in youth these days: since young folk have given up tending their betters. The remedy is sleep, and certain drugs,' said the Sahiba; and he was glad to give himself up to the blankness that half menaced and half soothed him.

She brewed drinks, in some mysterious Asiatic equivalent to the still-room – drenches that smelt pestilently and tasted worse. She stood over Kim till they went down, and inquired exhaustively after they had come up. She laid a taboo upon the forecourt, and enforced it by means of an armed man. It is true he was seventy odd, that his scab-barded sword ceased at the hilt; but he represented the authority of the Sahiba, and loaded wains, chattering servants, calves, dogs, hens, and the like, fetched a wide compass by those parts. Best of all, when the body was cleared, she cut out from the mass of poor relations that crowded the back of the buildings […] a cousin's widow, skilled in what Europeans, who know nothing about it, call massage. And the two of them, laying him east and west, that the mysterious earth-currents which thrill the clay of our bodies might help and not hinder, took him to pieces all one long afternoon – bone by bone, muscle by muscle, ligament by ligament, and lastly, nerve by nerve. Kneaded to irresponsible pulp, half hypnotized by the perpetual flick and read-justment of the uneasy chudders that veiled their eyes, Kim slid ten thousand miles into slumber – thirty-six hours of it – sleep that soaked like rain after drought.

Then she fed him, and the house spun to her clamour. She caused fowls to be slain; she sent for vegetables, and the sober, slow-thinking gardener, nigh as old as she, sweated for it; she took spices, and milk, and onion, with little fish from the brooks – anon limes for sherbets, fat quails from the pits, then chicken-livers upon a skewer, with sliced ginger between.

'I have seen something of this world,' she said over the crowded trays, 'and there are but two sorts of women in it – those who take the strength out of a man and those who put it back. Once I was that one, and now I am this. Nay – do not play the priestling with me. Mine was but a jest. If it does not hold good now, it will when thou takest the road again. Cousin,' – this to the poor relation, never wearied of extolling her patroness's charity – 'he is getting a bloom on the skin of a new-curried horse. Our work is like polishing jewels to be thrown to a dance-girl – eh?'

Kim sat up and smiled. The terrible weakness had dropped from him like an old shoe. His tongue itched for free speech again, and but a week back the lightest word clogged it like ashes. The pain in his neck (he must have caught it from the lama) had gone with the heavy dengue-aches and the evil taste in the mouth. The two old women, a little, but not much, more careful about their veils now, clucked as merrily as the hens that had entered pecking through the open door.

✕ A World of Frenzied Industry

Arnold Bennett (1867–1931) revelled in domestic practicalities, and once said that his secret ambition was to be the manager of a great hotel. His description of the enormous kitchens in his novel Imperial Palace *is based on his observations at the Savoy – his favourite place to eat.*

The kitchens of the Imperial Palace restaurant were on the same floor as the restaurant itself, and immediately adjoining it. You passed through an open door, hidden like a guilty secret from all the dining-tables, then up a very short corridor, and at one step you were in another and a different world: a super-heated world of steel glistening and dull, and bare wood, and food in mass raw and cooked, and bustle, and hurrying to and fro, and running to and fro, and calling and even raucous shouting in French and Italian: a world of frenzied industry, whose denizens had leisure and inclination for neither the measured eloquence nor the discreet deferential murmuring nor the correct and starched apparelling of the priests and acolytes of the restaurant. A world of racket, which racket, reverberating among metals and earth-enware, rose to the low ceilings and was bounced down again on to the low tables and up again and down again. A world without end, a vista of kitchens one behind the other, beyond the range of vision. The denizens were all clad in white, or what had been white that morning, and wore high white caps, with sometimes a soiled towel for kerchief loosely folded round the neck; professional attire, of which none would have permitted himself to be deprived.

The shock of the introduction into the Dantesque Latin micro-cosm, of the transition from indolent luxury to feverish labour, was shown in Gracie's features …

Then approached down the vista a youngish, plump, jolly man, not to be distinguished by his attire from anybody else.

He had heard by the inexplicable telegraph which functions in workshops that the Director was in the kitchen, with guests; and he was hurrying.

'Ah!' said Evelyn. 'Here's Planquet, the chef of chefs.'

The man arrived, bowing.

'Let me introduce Maître Planquet,' Evelyn began the ceremonial of presentation.

The master-cook protected himself against the hazards of contact with the extraneous world by a triple system of defence. Outermost came the cushion of his amiable jollity. Next, a cushion of punctilious decorum – obeisances, deferential smiles, handshakings, which expressed his formal sense of a great honour received; for he needed no one to tell him that only visitors of the highest importance would be introduced by the Director himself. Third, and innermost, a steel breastplate forged from the tremendous conviction that the kitchens of the Imperial Palace restaurant were the finest kitchens in the universe, and that he, Planquet, a Frenchman, was the head of the finest kitchens in the universe, and therefore the head of his ancient profession.

When he genially admitted, in response to a suggestion in French from alert Gracie, that he was a Frenchman from the South of France, his tone had in it a note of interrogation, implying: 'Surely you did not imagine that any but a Frenchman of the Midi could possibly be the head of my profession?' His tone also indicated a full appreciation of the fact that Gracie was an exceeding pretty woman. Behind the steel breastplate dwelt unseen the inviolable vital spark of that fragment of the divine which was the master's soul.

While Sir Henry vouchsafed to him in the way of preliminary small-talk that he and his daughter and Mr. Orcham were in the middle of dinner in the restaurant, his unregarding, twinkling gaze seemed negligently to recognise that a restaurant, and perhaps many floors of a hotel, might conceivably be existing somewhere beyond the frontier of the kitchens, and that these phenomena were a corollary of the kitchens – but merely a corollary.

'Ah!' said Gracie, over a dishful of many uncooked cutlets, meek and uniform among various dishfuls of the raw material of art. 'They have not yet acquired their individualities.'

The master gave her a sudden surprised glance of sympathetic approbation; and Evelyn knew that the master was saying to himself, as Evelyn was saying to himself: 'She is no ordinary woman, this!' And for an instant the Director felt jealous of the master, as though none but the Director had the right to perceive that Gracie was no ordinary woman. The master's demeanour changed, and henceforth he spoke to Gracie as to one to whom God had granted understanding. He escorted her to the enormous open fire of wood in front of which a row of once-feathered vertebrates were slowly revolving on a horizontal rod.

'We return always to the old methods, mademoiselle,' said he. 'Here in this kitchen we cook by electricity, by gas, by everything you wish, but for the *volaille* we return always to the old methods. Wood fire.'

The intense heat halted Gracie. The master, however, august showman, walked right into it, seized an iron spoon fit for supping with the devil, and, having scooped up an immense spoonful of the fat which had dripped drop by drop from the roasting birds, poured it tenderly over them, and so again and again. Then he came back with his jolly smile to Gracie, as cool as an explorer returning from the arctic zone.

'Nothing else is worth the old methods,' said he, and made a polite indifferent remark to Sir Henry.

But the next minute he was displaying, further up the vista, a modern machine for whipping cream. And later, ice-making by hand.

'The good method of a hundred years since.' Then, further, far from the frontier, in the very hinterland of the kitchens, was heard a roar of orders. Two loud-speakers suspended from a ceiling over a table!

'Yes,' the master admitted to Gracie's questioning, ironic look. 'It is bizarre, it is a little bizarre, this mixture. But what would you, mademoiselle?'

Two shabby young men were working like beavers beneath the loud-speakers and round about, occasionally bawling acknowledgments of receipt of orders to colleagues in some distant county of the master's kingdom.

The party went in and out of rooms hot and rooms cold, rooms large and rooms small, rooms crowded with industry and rooms where one man toiled delicately alone. And the master explained his cuisine to Gracie, as one artist explains an art to another artist who is ignorant but who has instinctive comprehension. Down by a spiral staircase into the bakery and the cakery. Up into an office with intent clerks and typewriters. And everywhere white employees raised eyes for a second to the Director and his wandering charges and the master, and dropped them again to their tasks.

✕ One Vast Prey to Raging Dyspepsia

In his distinctly partial preface to his wife Jessie's Handbook of Cookery *(1923), Joseph Conrad (1857–1924) argued that Jessie's honest recipes for Bubble and Squeak, Beef Tea and Potato Cones would have eased the way the West was won and should be preferred to quack nostrums.*

Of all the books produced since the most remote age by human talents and industry those only that treat of cooking are, from a moral point of view, above suspicion. The intention of every other piece of prose may be discussed and even mistrusted; but the purpose of a cookery book is one and unmistakable. Its object can conceivably be no other than to increase the happiness of mankind.

This general consideration, and also a feeling of affectionate interest with which I am accustomed to view all the actions of the writer, prompt me to set down these few words of introduction for her book. Without making myself responsible for her teaching (I own that I find it impossible to read through a cookery book), I come forward modestly but gratefully as a Living Example of her practice. That practice I pronounce most successful. It has been for many priceless years adding to the sum of my daily happiness.

Good cooking is a moral agent. By good cooking I mean the conscientious preparation of the simple food of everyday life, not the more or less skilful concoction of idle feasts and rare dishes. Conscientious cookery is an enemy to gluttony. The trained delicacy of the palate, like a cultivated delicacy of sentiment, stands in the way of unseemly excesses. The decency of our life is for a great part a matter of good taste, of the correct appreciation of what is fine in simplicity. The intimate influence of conscientious cooking by rendering easy the processes of digestion promotes the serenity of mind, the graciousness of thought, and that indulgent view of our neighbour's failings which is the only genuine form of optimism. Those are its titles to our reverence.

A great authority on the North American Indians accounted for the sombre and excessive ferocity characteristic of these savages by

the theory that as a race they suffered from perpetual indigestion. The noble Red Man was a mighty hunter, but his wives had not mastered the art of conscientious cookery. The Seven Nations around the Great Lakes an the Horse-tribes of the Plains were but one vast prey to raging dyspepsia. The noble Red Men were great warriors, great orators, great masters of outdoor pursuits; but the domestic life of their wigwams was clouded by the morose irritability which follows the consumption of ill-cooked food. The gluttony of their indigestible feasts was a direct incentive to counsels of unreasonable violence. Victims of gloomy imaginings, they lived in abject submission to the wiles of a multitude of fraudulent medicine men – quacks – who haunted their existence with vain promises and false nostrums from the cradle to the grave.

It is to be remarked that the quack of modern civilization, the vendor of patent medicine, preys mainly upon the races of Anglo-Saxon stock who are also great warriors, great orators, mighty hunters, great masters of outdoor pursuits. No virtue will avail for happiness if the righteous art of cookery be neglected by the national conscience. We owe much to the fruitful meditations of our sages, but a sane view of life is, after all, elaborated mainly in the kitchen – the kitchen of the small house, the abode of the preponderant majority of the people. And a sane view of life excludes the belief in patent medicine. The conscientious cook is the natural enemy of the quack without a conscience; and thus his labours make for the honesty, and favour the amenity, of our existence. For a sane view of life can be no other than kindly and joyous, but a believer in patent medicine is steeped in the gloom of vague fears, the sombre attendants of disordered digestion.

Strong in this conviction, I introduce this little book to the inhabitants of the little houses who are the arbiters of the nation's destiny. Ignorant of the value of its methods, I have no doubt whatever as to its intention. It is highly moral. There cannot be the slightest question as to that; for is it not a cookery book? – the only product of the human mind altogether above suspicion.

In that respect no more need, or indeed can, be said. As regards the practical intention, I gather that no more than the clear and concise exposition of elementary principles has been the author's aim. And this, too, is laudable, because modesty is a becoming virtue in an artist. It remains for me only to express the hope that by correctness of practice and soundness of precept this little book will be able to add to the cheerfulness of nations.

6 Distant Times and Places

They sailed to the Western Sea, they did,
To a land all covered with trees,
And they bought an Owl, and a useful Cart,
And a pound of Rice, and a Cranberry Tart,
And a hive of silvery Bees.
And they bought a Pig, and some green Jack-daws,
And a lovely Monkey with lollipop paws,
And forty bottles of Ring-Bo-Ree,
And no end of Stilton Cheese.

Edward Lear

✗ The Ancient of Days

Teleclides (fl. 430 BC) described a golden age of plenty in his play The Amphictyons, *of which only a fragment survives.*

I will, then, tell of the life of old which I provided for mortals. First, there was peace over all, like water over hands. The earth produced no terror and no disease; on the other hand, things needful came of their own accord. Every stream flowed with wine, barley-cakes strove with wheat-loaves for men's lips, beseeching that they be swallowed if men loved the whitest. Fishes would come to the house and bake themselves, then serve themselves on the tables. A river of broth, whirling hot slices of meat, would flow by the couches; conduits full of piquant sauces for the meat were close at hand for the asking, so that there was plenty for moistening a mouthful and swallowing it tender. On dishes there would be honey-cakes all sprinkled with spices, and roast thrushes served up with milk-cakes were flying into the gullet. The flat-cakes jostled each other at the jaws and set up a racket, the slaves would shoot dice with slices of tripe and paunch and liver. Men were fat in those days and every bit mighty giants.

✗ Seethed Tortoise

This description of an exotic feast laid out to tempt a soul to return is from Zhao Hun *(The Summons of the Soul), which appears in a collection of mainly second-century-BC poems called* Ch'u Tz'u *(translated by David Hawkes as* The Songs of the South*, 1959).*

O Soul, come back! Why should you go so far away?
All your household have come to do you honour:
All kinds of good food are ready:
Rice, broom-corn, early wheat mixed with yellow millet,
Bitter, salt, sour, hot and sweet:
There are dishes of all flavours.
Ribs of the fatted ox cooked tender and succulent;
Sour and bitter blended in the soup of Wu;
Stewed turtle and roast kid, served up with yam sauce;
Geese cooked in sour sauce, casseroled duck,
Fried flesh of the great crane;
Braised chicken, seethed tortoise,
High seasoned, but not to spoil the taste;
Fried honey cakes of rice-flour and malt sugar sweetmeats;
Jade-like wine, honey-flavoured, fills the winged cups;
Ice-cooled liquor, strained of impurities,
Clear wine, cool and refreshing;
Here are laid out the patterned ladles,
And here is sparkling wine.

✕ A Zodiacal Dinner

In AD 61, Petronius wrote his description of the self-made Trimalchio's wildly over-the-top feast to satirise the excesses of Romans at the time of Nero. (Adapted from William Burnaby's 1694 translation of The Satyricon)

We reclined, and slave boys from Alexandria poured water cooled with snow upon our hands, while others following attended to our feet and removed the hangnails with wonderful dexterity, nor were they silent even during this disagreeable operation, but they all kept singing at their work. I was desirous of finding out whether the whole household could sing, so I ordered a drink; a boy near at hand instantly repeated my order in a singsong voice fully as shrill, and whichever one you accosted did the same. You would not imagine that this was the dining-room of a private gentleman, but rather that it was an exhibition of pantomimes.

A very inviting relish was brought on, for by now all the couches were occupied save only that of Trimalchio, for whom the chief place was reserved. On the tray stood a donkey made of Corinthian bronze, bearing panniers containing olives, white in one and black in the other. Two platters flanked the figure, on the margins of which were engraved Trimalchio's name and the weight of the silver in each. Dormice sprinkled with poppy-seed and honey were served on little bridges soldered fast to the platter, and hot sausages on a silver grid-iron, underneath which were damson plums and pomegranate seeds.

We were in the midst of these delicacies when, to the sound of music, Trimalchio himself was carried in and bolstered up in a nest of small cushions, which forced a snicker from the less wary. A shaven poll protruded from a scarlet mantle, and around his neck, already muffled with heavy clothing, he had tucked a napkin having a broad purple stripe and a fringe that hung down all around. On the little finger of his left hand he wore a massive gilt ring, and on the first joint of the next finger, a smaller one which seemed to me to be of pure gold, but as a matter of fact it had iron stars soldered on all around it. And then, for fear all of his finery would not be displayed, he bared his right arm, adorned with a golden arm-band and an ivory circlet clasped with a plate of shining metal …

A tray was brought in, on which was a basket containing a wooden hen with her wings rounded and spread out as if she were brooding. Two slaves instantly approached, and to the accompaniment of music, commenced to feel around in the straw. They pulled out some pea-hen's eggs, which they distributed among the diners. Turning his head, Trimalchio saw what was going on. 'Friends,' he remarked. 'I ordered pea-hen's eggs set under the hen, but I'm afraid they're addled, by Hercules I am. Let's try them anyhow, and see if they're still fit to suck.' We picked up our silver spoons, each of which weighed not less than half a pound, and punctured the shells, which were made of flour and dough. As a matter of fact, I very nearly threw mine away for it seemed to me that a chick had formed already, but upon hearing an old experienced guest vow, 'There must be something good here,' I broke open the shell with my hand and discovered a fine fat fig-pecker, imbedded in a yolk seasoned with pepper.

Some glass bottles carefully sealed with gypsum were brought in at that instant; a label bearing this inscription was fastened to the neck of each one: Opimian Falernian: One Hundred Years Old. While we were studying the labels, Trimalchio clapped his hands and cried, 'Ah me! To think that wine lives longer than poor little man. Fill up! There's life in wine and this is the real Opimian, you can take my word for that.'

We were tippling away and extolling all these elegant devices, when a slave brought in a silver skeleton, so contrived that the joints and movable vertebrae could be turned in any direction. He threw it down upon the table a time or two, and its mobile articulation caused it to assume grotesque attitudes, whereupon Trimalchio chimed in: 'Poor man is nothing in the scheme of things. Orcus grips us and to Hades flings our bones! This skeleton before us here is as important as we ever were! Let's live then while we may; life is dear.'

Our applause was followed by a course which, by its oddity, drew every eye, but it did not come up to our expectations. There was a circular tray around which were displayed the signs of the zodiac, and upon each sign the caterer had placed the food best in keeping with it. Ram's head pease on Aries, a piece of beef on Taurus, kidneys and lamb's fry on Gemini, a crown on Cancer, the womb of an unfarrowed sow on Virgo, an African fig on Leo, on Libra a balance, one pan of

which held a tart and the other a cake, a small seafish on Scorpio, a bull's eye on Sagittarius, a sea lobster on Capricornus, a goose on Aquarius and two mullets on Pisces. In the middle lay a piece of cut turf upon which rested a honeycomb with the grass arranged around it. An Egyptian slave passed bread around from a silver oven and in a most discordant voice twisted out a song in the manner of the mime in the musical farce called Laserpitium. Seeing that we were rather depressed at the prospect of busying ourselves with such vile fare, Trimalchio urged us to fall to: 'Let us fall to, gentlemen, I beg of you, this is only the sauce!'

While he was speaking, four dancers ran in to the time of the music, and removed the upper part of the tray. Beneath, on what seemed to be another tray, we caught sight of stuffed capons and sows' bellies, and in the middle, a hare equipped with wings to resemble Pegasus. At the corners of the tray we also noted four figures of Marsyas and from their bladders spouted a highly spiced sauce upon fish which were swimming about as if in a tide-race. All of us echoed the applause which was started by the servants, and fell to upon these exquisite delicacies, with a laugh. 'Carver,' cried Trimalchio, no less delighted with the artifice practised upon us, and the carver appeared immediately. Timing his strokes to the beat of the music he cut up the meat in such a fashion as to lead you to think that a gladiator was fighting from a chariot to the accompaniment of a water-organ.

✗ Gorging at Pleasure

Gustave Flaubert (1821–1880) steeped himself in Carthaginian history in order to write his historical novel Salammbô *(1862). The book opens with this description of the riotous feast enjoyed in Hamilcar's absence by his soldiers in his gardens at Megara on the anniversary of the battle of Eryx. (Translated by JS Chartres, 1931)*

Hamilcar's kitchens being insufficient, the Council had sent them slaves, ware, and beds, and in the middle of the garden, as on a battle-field when they burn the dead, large bright fires might be seen, at which oxen were roasting. Anise-sprinkled loaves alternated with great cheeses heavier than discuses, crateras filled with wine, and cantharuses filled with water, together with baskets of gold filigree-work containing flowers. Every eye was dilated with the joy of being able at last to gorge at pleasure, and songs were beginning here and there.

First they were served with birds and green sauce in plates of red clay relieved by drawings in black, then with every kind of shell-fish that is gathered on the Punic coasts, wheaten porridge, beans and barley, and snails dressed with cumin on dishes of yellow amber.

Afterwards the tables were covered with meats, antelopes with their horns, peacocks with their feathers, whole sheep cooked in sweet wine, haunches of she-camels and buffaloes, hedgehogs with garum, fried grasshoppers, and preserved dormice. Large pieces of fat floated in the midst of saffron in bowls of Tamrapanni wood. Everything was running over with wine, truffles, and asafoetida. Pyramids of fruit were crumbling upon honeycombs, and they had not forgotten a few of those plump little dogs with pink silky hair and fattened on olive lees – a Carthaginian dish held in abhorrence among other nations. Surprise at the novel fare excited the greed of the stomach. The Gauls with their long hair drawn up on the crown of the head, snatched at the water-melons and lemons, and crunched them up with the rind. The Negroes, who had never seen a lobster, tore their faces with its red prickles. But the shaven Greeks, whiter than marble, threw the leavings of their plates behind them, while the herdsmen from Brutium, in their wolf-skin garments, devoured in silence with their faces in their portions.

Night fell. The velarium, spread over the cypress avenue, was drawn back, and torches were brought. The apes, sacred to the moon, were terrified on the cedar tops by the wavering lights of the petroleum as it burned in the porphyry vases. They uttered screams which afforded mirth to the soldiers.

Oblong flames trembled in cuirasses of brass. Every kind of scintillation flashed from the gem-incrusted dishes. The crateras with their borders of convex mirrors multiplied and enlarged the images of things; the soldiers thronged around, looking at their reflections with amazement, and grimacing to make themselves laugh. They tossed the ivory stools and golden spatulas to one another across the tables. They gulped down all the Greek wines in their leathern bottles, the Campanian wine enclosed in amphoras, the Cantabrian wines brought in casks, with the wines of the jujube, cinnamomum and lotus. There were pools of these on the ground that made the foot slip. The smoke of the meats ascended into the foliage with the vapour of the breath. Simultaneously were heard the snapping of jaws, the noise of speech, songs, and cups, the crash of Campanian vases shivering into a thousand pieces, or the limpid sound of a large silver dish. As their intoxication increased they more and more recalled the injustice of Carthage.

✕ Gulliver Eats a Laputian Feast

Jonathan Swift (1667–1745) offered political satire in the form of a parody of travel literature in his Gulliver's Travels *in 1726; later that year the poet John Gay wrote that it was 'universally read, from the cabinet council to the nursery'. Of all the styles of eating Gulliver experienced, the strangest was that of the mathematically minded inhabitants of the flying island of Laputa.*

At my alighting, I was surrounded with a crowd of people, but those who stood nearest seemed to be of better quality. They beheld me with all the marks and circumstances of wonder; neither indeed was I much in their debt, having never till then seen a race of mortals so singular in their shapes, habits, and countenances. Their heads were all reclined, either to the right, or the left; one of their eyes turned inward, and the other directly up to the zenith. Their outward garments were adorned with the figures of suns, moons, and stars; interwoven with those of fiddles, flutes, harps, trumpets, guitars, harpsichords, and many other instruments of music, unknown to us in Europe …

My dinner was brought, and four persons of quality, whom I remembered to have seen very near the king's person, did me the honour to dine with me. We had two courses, of three dishes each. In the first course, there was a shoulder of mutton cut into an equilateral triangle, a piece of beef into a rhomboides, and a pudding into a cycloid. The second course was two ducks trussed up in the form of fiddles; sausages and puddings resembling flutes and hautboys, and a breast of veal in the shape of a harp. The servants cut our bread into cones, cylinders, parallelograms, and several other mathematical figures.

While we were at dinner, I made bold to ask the names of several things in their language, and those noble persons, by the assistance of their flappers, delighted to give me answers, hoping to raise my admiration of their great abilities if I could be brought to converse with them. I was soon able to call for bread and drink, or whatever else I wanted.

✕ All the Refinements of Cookery

James Justinian Morier (1782–1849) lived in Persia for six years before writing The Adventures of Hajji Baba of Ispahan *(1824), a picaresque satire of its extravagant and corrupt government.*

The only persons, besides servants, admitted into the saloon, where the Shah dined, were the three princes, his sons, who had accompanied him; and they stood at the farthest end, with their backs against the wall, attired in dresses of ceremony.

Mirza Ahmek, his chief physician and host, remained in attendance without. A cloth of the finest Cashmerian shawl, fringed with gold, was then spread on the carpet before the king, and a gold ewer and basin was presented for washing hands. The dinner was then brought in trays, which, as a precaution against poison, had been sealed with the signet of the head steward before they left the kitchen, and were broken open by him again in the presence of the Shah.

Here were displayed all the refinements of cookery:

Rice, in various shapes, smoked upon the board; first, the chilau, as white as snow; then the pilau, with a piece of boiled lamb, smothered in the rice; then another pilau with a baked fowl in it; a fourth, coloured with saffron, mixed up with dried peas; and at length, the king of Persian dishes, the narinj pilau, made with slips of orange peel, spices of all sorts, almonds and sugar.

Salmon and herring, from the Caspian Sea, were seen among the dishes; and trout from the river Zengi; then in china basins and bowls of different sizes were the ragouts, which consisted of hash, made of a fowl boiled to rags, stewed with rice, sweet herbs and onions; a stew, in which was a lamb's marrow bone, with some loose flesh about it, and boiled in its own juice; small gourds, crammed with force-meat, and done in butter; a fowl stewed to rags, with a brown sauce of prunes; a large omelette, about two inches thick; a cup full of the essence of meat, mixed with rags of lamb, almonds, prunes and tamarinds, which was poured upon the top of the chilau; a plate of poached eggs, fried in butter and sugar, and a stew of venison. After these came the roasts.

A lamb was served up hot from the spit, the tail of which was curled up over its back. Partridges, and what is looked upon as the rarest delicacy in Persia, two partridges of the valley, were procured for the occasion. Pheasants from Mazanderan were there also, as well as some of the choicest bits of the wild ass and antelope.

The display and the abundance of delicacies surprised every one; and they were piled up in such profusion around the king, that he seemed almost to form a part of the heap. I do not mention the innumerable little accessories of preserves, pickles, cheese, butter, onions, celery, salt, pepper, sweets and sours, which were to be found in different parts of the tray, for that would be tedious; but the sherbets were worthy of notice, from their peculiar delicacy; these were contained in immense bowls of the most costly china, and drank by the help of spoons of the most exquisite workmanship, made of the pear-tree. They consisted of the common lemonade, made with superior art, of the sekenjabin or vinegar, sugar and water, so mixed that the sour and the sweet were as equally balanced as the blessings and miseries of life, the sherbet of sugar and water, with rose-water to give it a perfume, and sweet seeds to increase its flavour, and that made of the pomegranate; all highly cooled by lumps of floating ice.

The king, then doubling himself down, with his head reclining towards his food, buried his hand in the pilaus and other dishes before him, and ate in silence, while the princes and servants remained immovable. When he had finished, he got up, and walked into an adjoining room, where he washed his hands, drank his coffee, and smoked his water-pipe.

✂ The Rule Against Grog was Rescinded

While searching for a northerly route from the Atlantic to the Pacific in 1829–1830, the intrepid Sir John Ross (1777–1856) kept up his crew's spirits by celebrating Christmas dinner (From Narrative of a Second Voyage in Search of a North-West Pasasage, *1835.)*

December 25 (Christmas Day) 1829. The elements themselves seemed to have determined that it should be a noted day to us, for it commenced with a most beautiful and splendid aurora, occupying the whole vault above. At first, and for many hours, it displayed a succession of arches, gradually increasing in altitude as they advanced from the east and proceeded towards the western side of the horizon; while the succession of changes were not less brilliant than any that we had formerly witnessed.

The church service allotted for this peculiar day was adopted; but, as is the etiquette of the naval service, the holiday also kept by an unusually liberal dinner, of which, roast beef from our Galloway ox, not yet expended, formed the essential and orthodox portion. I need not say that the rule against grog was rescinded for this day, since, without that, it would not have been the holiday expected by a seaman. The stores of the *Fury* rendered us, here, even more than the reasonable service we might have claimed, since they included mince pies, and what would have been more appropriate elsewhere, though abundantly natural here, iced cherry brandy with its fruit; matters, however, of amusement, when we recollected that we were rioting in the luxuries of a hot London June, without the heat of a ball in Grosvenor Square to give them value, and really without any special desire for a sweetmeat of so cooling a nature. I believe that it was a happy day for all the crew: and happy days had a moral value with us, little suspected by those whose lives, of uniformity, and of uniform ease, peace, and luxury, one or all, render them as insensible to those hardwon enjoyments, as unobservant of their effects on the minds of men. To display all our flags was a matter of course; and the brilliancy of Venus was a spectacle which was naturally contemplated as in harmony with the rest of the day.

✕ A Succulent Dish of Fried Seal Liver?

Sir John Ross's feast compares interestingly with the 'Sketch of the Life at Hut Point' written by Captain Robert Falcon Scott (1868–1912) during his ill-fated expedition to the South Pole in 1910–1913. Although Ross's men dined better, the warm camaraderie of Scott and his fellows made up for culinary disaster.

We have picked up quite a number of fish frozen in the ice – the larger ones about the size of a herring and the smaller of a minnow. We imagined both had been driven into the slushy ice by seals, but today Gran found a large frozen fish in the act of swallowing a small one. It looks as if both small and large are caught when one is chasing the other.

We gather around the fire seated on packing-cases to receive them with a hunk of butter and a steaming pannikin of tea, and life is well worth living. After lunch we are out and about again; there is little to tempt a long stay indoors and exercise keeps us all the fitter.

The falling light and approach of supper drives us home again with good appetites about 5 or 6 o'clock, and then the cooks rival one another in preparing succulent dishes of fried seal liver. A single dish may not seem to offer much opportunity of variation, but a lot can be done with a little flour, a handful of raisins, a spoonful of curry powder, or the addition of a little boiled pea meal. Be this as it may, we never tire of our dish and exclamations of satisfaction can be heard every night – or nearly every night, for two nights ago [April 4] Wilson, who has proved a genius in the invention of 'plats', almost ruined his reputation.

He proposed to fry the seal liver in penguin blubber, suggesting that the latter could be freed from all rankness. The blubber was obtained and rendered down with great care, the result appeared as delightfully pure fat free from smell; but appearances were deceptive; the 'fry' proved redolent of penguin, a concentrated essence of that peculiar flavour which faintly lingers in the meat and should not be emphasised. Three heroes got through their pannikins, but the rest of us decided to be contented with cocoa and biscuit after tasting the first mouthful.

After supper we have an hour or so of smoking and conversation – a cheering, pleasant hour – in which reminiscences are exchanged by a company which has very literally had world-wide experience. There is scarce a country under the sun which one or another of us has not travelled in, so diverse are our origins and occupations. An hour or so after supper we tail off one by one, spread out our sleeping-bags, take off our shoes and creep into comfort, for our reindeer bags are really warm and comfortable now that they have had a chance of drying, and the hut retains some of the heat generated in it. Thanks to the success of the blubber lamps and to a fair supply of candles, we can muster ample light to read for another hour or two, and so tucked up in our furs we study the social and political questions of the past decade.

✕ Heart-Warming Food

The Scottish explorer of the Nile Dr David Livingstone (1813–1873) spent
many years in other parts of Africa as a medical missionary. Here he describes
the hospitality he received from the great Makololo chief Sekeletu.

When we arrived at any village the women all turned out to lulliloo
their chief. Their shrill voices, to which they give a tremulous sound
by a quick motion of the tongue, peal forth, 'Great lion!' 'Great chief!'
'Sleep, my lord!' etc. The men utter similar salutations; and Sekeletu
receives all with becoming indifference. After a few minutes' conversation and telling the news, the head man of the village, who is almost
always a Makololo, rises, and brings forth a number of large pots of
beer. Calabashes, being used as drinking-cups, are handed round, and
as many as can partake of the beverage do so, grasping the vessels so
eagerly that they are in danger of being broken.

They bring forth also large pots and bowls of thick milk; some
contain six or eight gallons; and each of these, as well as of the beer,
is given to a particular person, who has the power to divide it with
whom he pleases. The head man of any section of the tribe is generally selected for this office. Spoons not being generally in fashion, the
milk is conveyed to the mouth with the hand. I often presented my
friends with iron spoons, and it was curious to observe how their habit
of hand-eating prevailed, though they were delighted with the spoons.
They lifted out a little with the utensil, then put it on the left hand,
and ate it out of that.

As the Makololo have great abundance of cattle, and the chief is
expected to feed all who accompany him, he either selects an ox or
two of his own from the numerous cattle stations that he possesses at
different spots all over the country, or is presented by the head men
of the villages he visits with as many as he needs by way of tribute.
The animals are killed by a thrust from a small javelin in the region
of the heart, the wound being purposely small in order to avoid any
loss of blood, which, with the internal parts, are the perquisites of
the men who perform the work of the butcher; hence all are eager
to render service in that line. Each tribe has its own way of cutting

up and distributing an animal. Among the Makololo the hump and ribs belong to the chief; among the Bakwains the breast is his perquisite. After the oxen are cut up, the different joints are placed before Sekeletu, and he apportions them among the gentlemen of the party. The whole is rapidly divided by their attendants, cut into long strips, and so many of these are thrown into the fires at once that they are nearly put out. Half broiled and burning hot, the meat is quickly handed round; every one gets a mouthful, but no one except the chief has time to masticate. It is not the enjoyment of eating they aim at, but to get as much of the food into the stomach as possible during the short time the others are cramming as well as themselves, for no one can eat more than a mouthful after the others have finished. They are eminently gregarious in their eating; and, as they despise any one who eats alone, I always poured out two cups of coffee at my own meals, so that the chief, or some one of the principal men, might partake along with me. They all soon become very fond of coffee; and, indeed, some of the tribes attribute greater fecundity to the daily use of this beverage. They were all well acquainted with the sugar-cane, as they cultivate it in the Barotse country, but knew nothing of the method of extracting the sugar from it. They use the cane only for chewing. Sekeletu, relishing the sweet coffee and biscuits, of which I then had a store, said 'he knew my heart loved him by finding his own heart warming to my food.' He had been visited during my absence at the Cape by some traders and Griquas, and 'their coffee did not taste half so nice as mine, because they loved his ivory and not himself.' This was certainly an original mode of discerning character.

✕ Chowder at the Try Pots Inn

Herman Melville (1819–1891) used his own experiences on a five-year voyage on the whaling ship Acushnet *to inform his epic romance* Moby-Dick *(1851). In Chapter 15, Ishmael and Queequeg discover a 'surpassingly excellent' version of the Nantucket seafood stew known as chowder.*

It was quite late in the evening when the little *Moss* came snugly to anchor, and Queequeg and I went ashore; so we could attend to no business that day, at least none but a supper and a bed. The landlord of the Spouter Inn had recommended us to his cousin Hosea Hussey of the Try Pots, whom he asserted to be the proprietor of one of the best kept hotels in all Nantucket, and moreover he had assured us that Cousin Hosea, as he called him, was famous for his chowders … By dint of beating about a little in the dark, and now and then knocking up a peaceable inhabitant to inquire the way, we at last came to something which there was no mistaking.

Two enormous wooden pots painted black, and suspended by asses' ears, swung from the cross-trees of an old top-mast, planted in front of an old doorway. The horns of the cross-trees were sawed off on the other side, so that this old top-mast looked not a little like a gallows. Perhaps I was over sensitive to such impressions at the time, but I could not help staring at this gallows with a vague misgiving. A sort of crick was in my neck as I gazed up to the two remaining horns; yes, two of them, one for Queequeg, and one for me. It's ominous, thinks I. A Coffin my innkeeper upon landing in my first whaling port; tombstones staring at me in the whalemen's chapel; and here a gallows! and a pair of prodigious black pots too! Are these last throwing out oblique hints touching Tophet?

I was called from these reflections by the sight of a freckled woman with yellow hair and a yellow gown, standing in the porch of the inn, under a dull red lamp swinging there, that looked much like an injured eye, and carrying on a brisk scolding with a man in a purple woollen shirt.

'Get along with ye,' said she to the man, 'or I'll be combing ye!'

'Come on, Queequeg,' said I, 'There's Mrs Hussey …'

Upon making known our desires for a supper and a bed, Mrs. Hussey ushered us into a little room, and seating us at a table spread with the relics of a recently concluded repast, turned round to us and said – 'Clam or Cod?'

'What's that about Cods, ma'am?' said I, with much politeness.

'Clam or Cod?' she repeated.

'A clam for supper? a cold clam; is that what you mean, Mrs. Hussey?' says I; 'but that's a rather cold and clammy reception in the winter time, ain't it, Mrs Hussey?'

But being in a great hurry … and seeming to hear nothing but the word 'clam,' Mrs. Hussey hurried towards an open door leading to the kitchen, and bawling out 'clam for two,' disappeared.

'Queequeg,' said I, 'do you think that we can make out a supper for us both on one clam?'

However, a warm savoury steam from the kitchen served to belie the apparently cheerless prospect before us. But when that smoking chowder came in, the mystery was delightfully explained. Oh, sweet friends! hearken to me. It was made of small juicy clams, scarcely bigger than hazel nuts, mixed with pounded ship biscuit, and salted pork cut up into little flakes; the whole enriched with butter, and plentifully seasoned with pepper and salt. Our appetites being sharpened by the frosty voyage, and in particular, Queequeg seeing his favorite fishing food before him, and the chowder being surpassingly excellent, we despatched it with great expedition: when leaning back a moment and bethinking me of Mrs. Hussey's clam and cod announcement, I thought I would try a little experiment. Stepping to the kitchen door, I uttered the word 'cod' with great emphasis, and resumed my seat. In a few moments the savoury steam came forth again, but with a different flavour, and in good time a fine cod-chowder was placed before us.

We resumed business; and while plying our spoons in the bowl, thinks I to myself, I wonder now if this here has any effect on the head? What's that stultifying saying about chowder-headed people? 'But look, Queequeg, ain't that a live eel in your bowl? Where's your harpoon?'

Fishiest of all fishy places was the Try Pots, which well deserved its name; for the pots there were always boiling chowders. Chowder for breakfast, and chowder for dinner, and chowder for supper, till you began to look for fish-bones coming through your clothes. The area before the house was paved with clam-shells. Mrs. Hussey wore a polished necklace of codfish vertebra; and Hosea Hussey had his account books bound in superior old shark-skin. There was a fishy flavor to the milk, too, which I could not at all account for, till one morning happening to take a stroll along the beach among some fishermen's boats, I saw Hosea's brindled cow feeding on fish remnants, and marching along the sand with each foot in a cod's decapitated head, looking very slip-shod, I assure ye.

Supper concluded, we received a lamp, and directions from Mrs. Hussey concerning the nearest way to bed; but, as Queequeg was about to precede me up the stairs, the lady reached forth her arm, and demanded his harpoon; she allowed no harpoon in her chambers. 'Why not?' said I; 'every true whaleman sleeps with his harpoon – but why not?' 'Because it's dangerous,' says she. 'Ever since young Stiggs coming from that unfort'nt v'y'ge of his, when he was gone four years and a half, with only three barrels of ile, was found dead in my first floor back, with his harpoon in his side; ever since then I allow no boarders to take sich dangerous weepons in their rooms at night. So, Mr. Queequeg' (for she had learned his name), 'I will just take this here iron, and keep it for you till morning. But the chowder; clam or cod to-morrow for breakfast, men?'

'Both,' says I; 'and let's have a couple of smoked herring by way of variety.'

✗ A Dash of the Epicure

The Ebb-Tide (1894) was the last book written by Robert Louis Stevenson (1850–1894); his stepson Lloyd Osbourne (1868–1947) was credited as co-author. A gory tale of no-goods who invade the Pacific paradise of Attwater, an English harvester of pearls, it uses the dinner to which he invites them to point up a contrast between his hospitality and their fell intent. But Attwater is far from being gullible.

'Well, shall we step on the verandah? I have a dry sherry that I would like your opinion of.'

Herrick followed him forth to where, under the light of the hanging lamps, the table shone with napery and crystal; followed him as the criminal goes with the hangman, or the sheep with the butcher; took the sherry mechanically, drank it, and spoke mechanical words of praise. The object of his terror had become suddenly inverted; till then he had seen Attwater trussed and gagged, a helpless victim, and had longed to run in and save him; he saw him now tower up mysterious and menacing, the angel of the Lord's wrath, armed with knowledge and threatening judgment. He set down his glass again, and was surprised to see it empty.

'You go always armed?' he said, and the next moment could have plucked his tongue out.

'Always,' said Attwater. 'I have been through a mutiny here; that was one of my incidents of missionary life.'

And just then the sound of voices reached them, and looking forth from the verandah they saw Huish and the captain drawing near.

They sat down to an island dinner, remarkable for its variety and excellence; turtle soup and steak, fish, fowls, a sucking pig, a cocoanut salad, and sprouting cocoanut roasted for dessert. Not a tin had been opened; and save for the oil and vinegar in the salad, and some green spears of onion which Attwater cultivated and plucked with his own hand, not even the condiments were European. Sherry, hock, and claret succeeded each other, and the Farallone champagne brought up the rear with the dessert.

It was plain that, like so many of the extremely religious in the days before teetotalism, Attwater had a dash of the epicure. For such characters it is softening to eat well; doubly so to have designed and had prepared an excellent meal for others; and the manners of their host were agreeably mollified in consequence.

A cat of huge growth sat on his shoulders purring, and occasionally, with a deft paw, capturing a morsel in the air. To a cat he might be likened himself, as he lolled at the head of his table, dealing out attentions and innuendoes, and using the velvet and the claw indifferently. And both Huish and the captain fell progressively under the charm of his hospitable freedom …

'Well, now, see 'ere!' said Huish. 'You have everything about you in no end style, and no mistake, but I tell you it wouldn't do for me. Too much of "the old rustic bridge by the mill"; too retired, by 'alf. Give me the sound of Bow Bells!'

'You must not think it was always so,' replied Attwater, 'This was once a busy shore, although now, hark! you can hear the solitude. I find it stimulating. And talking of the sound of bells, kindly follow a little experiment of mine in silence.' There was a silver bell at his right hand to call the servants; he made them a sign to stand still, struck the bell with force, and leaned eagerly forward. The note rose clear and strong; it rang out clear and far into the night and over the deserted island; it died into the distance until there only lingered in the porches of the ear a vibration that was sound no longer. 'Empty houses, empty sea, solitary beaches!' said Attwater. 'And yet God hears the bell! And yet we sit in this verandah on a lighted stage with all heaven for spectators! And you call that solitude?'

7 Simple Pleasures

When I drink tea, I am conscious of peace.
the cool breath of heaven rises in
my sleeve and blows my cares away.

Lo Tong

Gentle baker, make good bread! For good bread
doth comfort, and doth establish a man's heart.

Andrew Boorde

Breadmaking is one of those almost hypnotic
businesses, like a dance from some ancient
ceremony. It leaves you filled with one of the
world's sweetest smells.

MFK Fisher

✕ Exceedingly Graceful

*The essayist Charles Lamb (1775–1834) argues that saying grace is best suited to simple meals (*Essays of Elia*, 1823).*

The custom of saying grace at meals had, probably, its origin in the early times of the world, and the hunter-state of man, when dinners were precarious things, and a full meal was something more than a common blessing; when a bellyful was a windfall, and looked like a special providence. In the shouts and triumphal songs with which, after a season of sharp abstinence, a lucky booty of deer's or goat's flesh would naturally be ushered home, existed, perhaps, the germ of the modern grace. It is not otherwise easy to be understood, why the blessing of food – the act of eating – should have had a particular expression of thanksgiving annexed to it, distinct from that implied and silent gratitude with which we are expected to enter upon the enjoyment of the many other various gifts and good things of existence.

I own that I am disposed to say grace upon twenty other occasions in the course of the day, besides my dinner. I want a form for setting out upon a pleasant walk, for a moonlight ramble, for a friendly meeting, or a solved problem. Why have we none for books, those spiritual repasts – a grace before Milton – a grace before Shakespeare – a devotional exercise proper to be said before reading The Faerie Queen? – but, the received ritual having prescribed these forms to the solitary ceremony of manducation [eating], I shall confine my observations to the experience which I have had of the grace, properly so called …

The form then of the benediction before eating has its beauty at a poor man's table, or at the simple and unprovocative repasts of children. It is here that the grace becomes exceedingly graceful. The indigent man, who hardly knows whether he shall have a meal the next day or not, sits down to his fare with a present sense of the blessing, which can be but feebly acted by the rich, into whose minds the conception of wanting a dinner could never, but by some extreme theory, have entered. The proper end of food – the animal sustenance – is barely contemplated by them. The poor man's bread is his daily bread, literally his bread for the day. Their courses are perennial.

Again, the plainest diet seems the fittest to be preceded by the grace. That which is least stimulative to appetite, leaves the mind the most free for foreign considerations. A man may feel thankful, heartily thankful, over a dish of plain mutton with turnips, and have leisure to reflect upon the ordinance and institution of eating; when he shall confess a perturbation of mind, inconsistent with the purposes of the grace, at the presence of venison or turtle.

When I have sat (a *rarus hospes*) at rich men's tables, with the savoury soup and messes steaming up the nostrils, and moistening the lips of the guests with desire and a distracted choice, I have felt the introduction of that ceremony to be unseasonable. With the ravenous orgasm upon you, it seems impertinent to interpose a religious sentiment. It is a confusion of purpose to mutter out praises from a mouth that waters. The heats of epicurism put out the gentle flame of devotion. The incense which rises round is pagan, and the belly-god intercepts it for his own. The very excess of the provision beyond the needs, takes away all sense of proportion between the end and means. The giver is veiled by his gifts. You are startled at the injustice of returning thanks – for what? – for having too much, while so many starve. It is to praise the gods amiss.

✄ Only the Spiritual Parts of the Tea

The Closet of the Eminently Learned Sir Kenelm Digby Opened was *first published in 1669. This unusual recipe for tea mixed with egg yolks and sugar dates from the early decades of the popularity of tea in England.*

The Jesuit that came from China, Anno Domini 1664, told Mr. Waller, that there they use sometimes in this manner. To near a pint of the infusion, take two yolks of new laid-eggs, and beat them very well with as much fine Sugar as is sufficient for this quantity of Liquor; when they are very well incorporated, pour your Tea upon the Eggs and Sugar, and stir them well together. So drink it hot.

This is when you come home from attending business abroad, and are very hungry, and yet have not conveniency to eat presently a competent meal. This presently discusseth and satisfieth all rawness and indigence of the stomach, flyeth suddenly over the whole body and into the veins, and strengtheneth exceedingly, and preserves one a good while from necessity of eating.

Mr. Waller findeth all those effects of it thus with Eggs. In these parts, he saith, we let the hot water remain too long soaking upon the Tea, which makes it extract into itself the earthy parts of the herb. The water is to remain upon it, no longer that whiles you can say the *Miserere* Psalm very leisurely. Then pour it upon the sugar, or sugar and Eggs. Thus you have only the spiritual parts of the Tea, which is much more active, penetrative and friendly to nature. You may from this regard take a little more of the herb; about one dram of Tea, will serve for a pint of water; which makes three ordinary draughts.

Nectareous Tides of Milk and Cream

The Scottish novelist Tobias Smollett (1721–1771) satirised high society in his last novel, The Expedition of Humphry Clinker *(1771). Here Matthew Bramble rhapsodises on the simplicity of life in the country.*

At Brambleton Hall, I have elbow room within doors, and breathe a clear, elastic, salutary air. I enjoy refreshing sleep, which is never disturbed by horrid noise, nor interrupted, but in a morning, by the sweet titter of the martlet at my window. I drink the virgin lymph, pure and crystalline as it gushes from the rock, or the sparkling beverage, home-brewed from malt of my own making; or I indulge with cider, which my own orchard affords, or with claret of the best growth, imported for my own use by a correspondent on whose integrity I can depend; my bread is sweet and nourishing, made from my own wheat, ground in my own mill, and baked in my own oven; my table is, in a great measure, furnished from my own ground; my five-year-old mutton, fed on the fragrant herbage of the mountains, that might vie with venison in juice and flavor; my delicious veal, fattened with nothing but the mother's milk, that fills the dish with gravy; my poultry from the barn door that never knew confinement but when they were at roost; my rabbits panting from the warren; my game fresh from the moors; my trout and salmon struggling from the stream; oysters from their native banks; and herrings, with other sea fish, I can eat in four hours after they are taken.

My salads, roots, and potherbs, my own garden yields in plenty and perfection, the produce of the natural soil, prepared by moderate cultivation. The same soil affords all the different fruits which England may call her own, so that my dessert is every day fresh gathered from the tree; my dairy flows with nectareous tides of milk and cream, from whence we derive abundance of excellent butter, curds, and cheese; and the refuse fattens my pigs, that are destined for hams and bacon. I go to bed betimes, and rise with the sun.

K

Kitchen Stuff

✕ Incomparably Good Toast

Karl Philipp Moritz, author of Travels in England in 1782, *was born in Hamelin in 1756 and died in 1793. Observant and optimistic, he walked England on a modest budget with a pocket edition of* Paradise Lost, *which he wanted to read 'in the land of Milton'.*

That same influenza which I left at Berlin, I have had the hard fortune again to find here; and many people die of it. It is as yet very cold for the time of the year, and I am obliged every day to have a fire. I must own that the heat or warmth given by sea-coal, burnt in the chimney, appears to me softer and milder than that given by our stoves. The sight of the fire has also a cheerful and pleasing effect. Only you must take care not to look at it steadily, and for a continuance, for this is probably the reason that there are so many young old men in England, who walk and ride in the public streets with their spectacles on; thus anticipating, in the bloom of youth, those conveniences and comforts which were intended for old age.

I now constantly dine in my own lodgings; and I cannot but flatter myself that my meals are regulated with frugality. My usual dish at supper is some pickled salmon, which you eat in the liquor in which it is pickled, along with some oil and vinegar; and he must be prejudiced or fastidious who does not relish it as singularly well tasted and grateful food …

The fine wheaten bread which I find here, besides excellent butter and Cheshire-cheese, makes up for my scanty dinners. For an English dinner, to such lodgers as I am, generally consists of a piece of half-boiled, or half-roasted meat; and a few cabbage leaves boiled in plain water; on which they pour a sauce made of flour and butter. This, I assure you, is the usual method of dressing vegetables in England.

The slices of bread and butter, which they give you with your tea, are as thin as poppy leaves. But there is another kind of bread and butter usually eaten with tea, which is toasted by the fire, and is incomparably good. You take one slice after the other and hold it to the fire on a fork till the butter is melted, so that it penetrates a number of slices at once: this is called Toast.

✗ The Smell Simply Talked to Toad

*Toast again: Kenneth Grahame (1859–1932) reputedly put something of his own son's character into Toad, including, I suspect, the small boy's love of toast and honey (*The Wind in the Willows, *1908).*

When the girl returned, some hours later, she carried a tray, with a cup of fragrant tea steaming on it; and a plate piled up with very hot buttered toast, cut thick, very brown on both sides, with the butter running through the holes in it in great golden drops, like honey from the honey-comb. The smell of that buttered toast simply talked to Toad, and with no uncertain voice; talked of warm kitchens, of break-fasts on bright frosty mornings, of cosy parlour firesides on winter evenings, when one's ramble was over and slippered feet were propped on the fender; of the purring of contented cats, and the twitter of sleepy canaries. Toad sat up on end once more, dried his eyes, sipped his tea and munched his toast.

✖ A Radish and an Egg

In his long narrative poem The Task, *William Cowper (1731–1800) paints his famous word picture of a tea taken around the hearth on a winter evening followed by a frugal supper.*

Now stir the fire, and close the shutters fast,
Let fall the curtains, wheel the sofa round,
And, while the bubbling and loud-hissing urn
Throws up a steamy column, and the cups,
That cheer but not inebriate, wait on each,
So let us welcome peaceful ev'ning in …
Here the needle plies its busy task,
The pattern grows, the well-depicted flow'r,
Wrought patiently into the snowy lawn,
Unfolds its bosom; buds, and leaves, and sprigs,
And curling tendrils, gracefully dispos'd,
Follow the nimble finger of the fair;
A wreath that cannot fade, or flow'rs that blow
With most success when all besides decay.
The poet's or historian's page, by one
Made vocal for th' amusement of the rest;
The sprightly lyre, whose treasure of sweet sounds
The touch from many a trembling chord shakes out;
And the clear voice symphonious, yet distinct,
And in the charming strife triumphant still,
Beguile the night, and set a keener edge
On female industry; the threaded steel
Flies swiftly, and unfelt the task proceeds.
The volume clos'd, the customary rites
Of the last meal commence. A Roman meal;
Such as the mistress of the world once found
Delicious, when her patriots of high note,
Perhaps by moonlight, at their humble doors,
And under an old oak's domestic shade,
Enjoy'd, spare feast! a radish and an egg.

✕ Let Onion Atoms Lurk

Sydney Smith (1771–1845) is famous for his versified recipe for a simple salad dressing. This is his own, later, version of the poem. It has more anchovy sauce and less onion than the one usually quoted.

Two large potatoes, passed through kitchen sieve,
Unwonted softness to the salad give.
Of mordant mustard add a single spoon,
Distrust the condiment that bites so soon;
But deem it not, thou man of herbs, a fault
To add a double quantity of salt.
Three times the spoon with oil from Lucca crown,
And once with vinegar procured from town.
True flavour needs it, and your poet begs
The pounded yellow of two well-boiled eggs;
Let onion atoms lurk within the bowl,
And, scarce suspected, animate the whole.
And, lastly, on the flavoured compound toss
A magic teaspoon of anchovy sauce.
Then though green turtle fail, though venison's tough.
And ham and turkey are not boiled enough.
Serenely full, the epicure may say,
'Fate cannot harm me, I have dined today.'

To Raise a Salad in Two Hours

No salad to dress? Of all the recipes offered by the esteemed eighteenth-century cook Hannah Glasse (1708–1770), nothing is simpler or more startling than this recipe for instant fresh salad (The Art of Cookery Made Plain and Easy, 1747). I dare you to try it.

Take fresh horse-dung hot, lay it in a tub near the fire, then sprinkle some mustard-seeds thick on it, lay a thin layer of horse-dung over it, cover it close and keep it by the fire, and it will rise high enough to cut in two hours.

Smoking and Tender and Juicy

William Thackeray (1811–1863) wrote his 'Ad Ministram' as a playful adaptation of 'Persicos Odi', an ode by Horace that deplores Persian luxuries and pleads for simplicity.

Dear LUCY, you know what my wish is, –
I hate all your Frenchified fuss:
Your silly entrées and made dishes
Were never intended for us.
No footman in lace and in ruffles
Need dangle behind my arm-chair;
And never mind seeking for truffles,
Although they be ever so rare.

But a plain leg of mutton, my Lucy,
I prithee get ready at three:
Have it smoking, and tender and juicy,
And what better meat can there be?
And when it has feasted the master,
'Twill amply suffice for the maid;
Meanwhile I will smoke my canaster,
And tipple my ale in the shade.

✕ Tea on the River

Jerome K Jerome (1859–1927) could not only make his readers laugh; he was also a master of the art of atmosphere. This description of a simple supper will appeal to all who enjoy messing about on the river.

We cleared the decks, and got out supper. We put the kettle on to boil, up in the nose of the boat, and went down to the stern and pretended to take no notice of it, but set to work to get the other things out.

That is the only way to get a kettle to boil up the river. If it sees that you are waiting for it and are anxious, it will never even sing. You have to go away and begin your meal, as if you were not going to have any tea at all. You must not even look round at it. Then you will soon hear it sputtering away, mad to be made into tea.

It is a good plan, too, if you are in a great hurry, to talk very loudly to each other about how you don't need any tea, and are not going to have any. You get near the kettle, so that it can overhear you, and then you shout out, 'I don't want any tea; do you, George?' to which George shouts back, 'Oh, no, I don't like tea; we'll have lemonade instead – tea's so indigestible.' Upon which the kettle boils over, and puts the stove out.

We adopted this harmless bit of trickery, and the result was that, by the time everything else was ready, the tea was waiting. Then we lit the lantern, and squatted down to supper.

We wanted that supper.

For five-and-thirty minutes not a sound was heard throughout the length and breadth of that boat, save the clank of cutlery and crockery, and the steady grinding of four sets of molars. At the end of five-and-thirty minutes, Harris said, 'Ah!' and took his left leg out from under him and put his right one there instead.

Five minutes afterwards, George said, 'Ah!' too, and threw his plate out on the bank; and, three minutes later than that, Montmorency gave the first sign of contentment he had exhibited since we had started, and rolled over on his side, and spread his legs out; and then I said, 'Ah!' and bent my head back, and bumped it against one of the hoops, but I did not mind it. I did not even swear.

How good one feels when one is full – how satisfied with ourselves and with the world! People who have tried it, tell me that a clear conscience makes you very happy and contented; but a full stomach does the business quite as well, and is cheaper, and more easily obtained. One feels so forgiving and generous after a substantial and well-digested meal – so noble-minded, so kindly-hearted.

It is very strange, this domination of our intellect by our digestive organs. We cannot work, we cannot think, unless our stomach wills so. It dictates to us our emotions, our passions. After eggs and bacon, it says, 'Work!' After beefsteak and porter, it says, 'Sleep!' After a cup of tea (two spoonsful for each cup, and don't let it stand more than three minutes), it says to the brain, 'Now, rise, and show your strength. Be eloquent, and deep, and tender; see, with a clear eye, into Nature and into life; spread your white wings of quivering thought, and soar, a god-like spirit, over the whirling world beneath you, up through long lanes of flaming stars to the gates of eternity!'

After hot muffins, it says, 'Be dull and soulless, like a beast of the field – a brainless animal, with listless eye, unlit by any ray of fancy, or of hope, or fear, or love, or life.' And after brandy, taken in suffi-cient quantity, it says, 'Now, come, fool, grin and tumble, that your fellow-men may laugh – drivel in folly, and splutter in senseless sounds, and show what a helpless ninny is poor man whose wit and will are drowned, like kittens, side by side, in half an inch of alcohol.'

We are but the veriest, sorriest slaves of our stomach. Reach not after morality and righteousness, my friends; watch vigilantly your stomach, and diet it with care and judgment. Then virtue and content-ment will come and reign within your heart, unsought by any effort of your own; and you will be a good citizen, a loving husband, and a tender father – a noble, pious man.

Before our supper, Harris and George and I were quarrelsome and snappy and ill-tempered; after our supper, we sat and beamed on one another, and we beamed upon the dog, too. We loved each other, we loved everybody. Harris, in moving about, trod on George's corn. Had this happened before supper, George would have expressed wishes and desires concerning Harris's fate in this world and the next that would have made a thoughtful man shudder.

As it was, he said: 'Steady, old man; 'ware wheat.'

And Harris, instead of merely observing, in his most unpleasant tones, that a fellow could hardly help treading on some bit of George's foot, if he had to move about at all within ten yards of where George was sitting, suggesting that George never ought to come into an ordinary sized boat with feet that length, and advising him to hang them over the side, as he would have done before supper, now said: 'Oh, I'm so sorry, old chap; I hope I haven't hurt you.'

And George said: 'Not at all;' that it was his fault; and Harris said no, it was his.

It was quite pretty to hear them.

We lit our pipes, and sat, looking out on the quiet night, and talked.

⚔ The Altruism of Oysters

James I is credited with having said 'He was a very valiant man who first adventured on an oyster'; in Charles Dickens' day, they were a popular dish with the poor. But by the time Hector Hugh Munro (1870–1916) wrote his dryly witty short stories under the pen-name of Saki, they were much esteemed as a simple luxury. This is from 'The Match-Maker'.

The grill-room clock struck eleven with the respectful unobtrusiveness of one whose mission in life is to be ignored … Six minutes later Clovis approached the supper-table, in the blessed expectancy of one who has dined sketchily and long ago.

'I'm starving,' he announced, making an effort to sit down gracefully and read the menu at the same time.

'So I gathered,' said his host, 'from the fact that you were nearly punctual. I ought to have told you that I'm a Food Reformer. I've ordered two bowls of bread-and-milk and some health biscuits. I hope you don't mind.'

Clovis pretended afterwards that he didn't go white above the collar-line for the fraction of a second.

'All the same,' he said, 'you ought not to joke about such things. There really are such people. I've known people who've met them. To think of all the adorable things there are to eat in the world, and then to go through life munching sawdust and being proud of it.'

'They're like the Flagellants of the Middle Ages, who went about mortifying themselves.'

'They had some excuse,' said Clovis. 'They did it to save their immortal souls, didn't they? You needn't tell me that a man who doesn't love oysters and asparagus and good wines has got a soul, or a stomach either. He's simply got the instinct for being unhappy highly developed.'

Clovis relapsed for a few golden moments into tender intimacies with a succession of rapidly disappearing oysters.

'I think oysters are more beautiful than any religion,' he resumed presently. 'They not only forgive our unkindness to them; they justify it, they incite us to go on being perfectly horrid to them. Once they

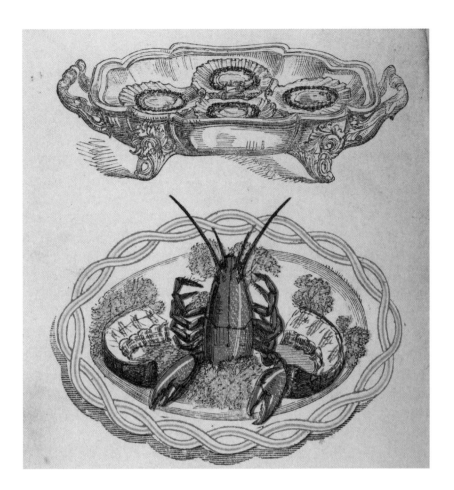

arrive at the supper-table they seem to enter thoroughly into the spirit of the thing. There's nothing in Christianity or Buddhism that quite matches the sympathetic unselfishness of an oyster.'

✗ A Shudder Ran Through My Whole Body

*No food anthology can omit Marcel Proust's (1871–1922) famous recollection of past times while sopping a Madeleine in tea (*Swann's Way, *translated by CK Scott Moncrieff).*

One day in winter, as I came home, my mother, seeing that I was cold, offered me some tea, a thing I did not ordinarily take. I declined at first, and then, for no particular reason, changed my mind. She sent out for one of those short, plump little cakes called 'petites madeleines,' which look as though they had been moulded in the fluted scallop of a pilgrim's shell. And soon, mechanically, weary after a dull day with the prospect of a depressing morrow, I raised to my lips a spoonful of the tea in which I had soaked a morsel of the cake. No sooner had the warm liquid, and the crumbs with it, touched my palate, than a

shudder ran through my whole body, and I stopped, intent upon the extraordinary changes that were taking place. An exquisite pleasure had invaded my senses, but individual, detached, with no suggestion of its origin. And at once the vicissitudes of life had become indifferent to me, its disasters innocuous, its brevity illusory – this new sensation having had on me the effect which love has of filling me with a precious essence; or rather this essence was not in me, it was myself. I had ceased now to feel mediocre, accidental, mortal. Whence could it have come to me, this all-powerful joy? I was conscious that it was connected with the taste of tea and cake, but that it infinitely transcended those savours, could not, indeed, be of the same nature as theirs. Whence did it come? What did it signify? How could I seize upon and define it?

I drink a second mouthful, in which I find nothing more than in the first, a third, which gives me rather less than the second. It is time to stop; the potion is losing its magic. It is plain that the object of my quest, the truth, lies not in the cup but in myself. The tea has called up in me, but does not itself understand, and can only repeat indefinitely with a gradual loss of strength, the same testimony; which I, too, cannot interpret, though I hope at least to be able to call upon the tea for it again and to find it there presently, intact and at my disposal, for my final enlightenment.

✗ Thank God for My Good Dinner

Flora Thompson (1876–1947) affectionately describes the rituals of the simple but nourishing daily meal taken by the farming families of Lark Rise *(1939).*

Here, then, were the three chief ingredients of the one hot meal a day, bacon from the flitch, vegetables from the garden, and flour for the roly-poly. This meal, called 'tea', was taken in the evening, when the men were home from the fields and the children from school, for neither could get home at midday.

About four o'clock, smoke would go up from the chimneys, as the fire was made up and the big iron boiler, or the three-legged pot, was slung on the hook of the chimney-chain. Everything was cooked in the one utensil; the square of bacon, amounting to little more than a taste each; cabbage, or other green vegetables in one net, potatoes in another, and the roly-poly swathed in a cloth. It sounds a haphazard method in these days of gas and electric cookers; but it answered its purpose, for, by carefully timing the putting in of each item and keeping the simmering of the pot well regulated, each item was kept intact and an appetising meal was produced. The water in which the food had been cooked, the potato parings, and other vegetable trimmings were the pig's share.

When the men came home from work they would find the table spread with a clean whitey-brown cloth, upon which would be knives and two-pronged steel forks with buckhorn handles. The vegetables would then be turned out into big round yellow crockery dishes and the bacon cut into dice, with much the largest cube upon Father's plate, and the whole family would sit down to the chief meal of the day. True, it was seldom that all could find places at the central table; but some of the smaller children could sit upon stools with the seat of a chair for a table, or on the doorstep with their plates on their laps.

Good manners prevailed. The children were given their share of the food, there was no picking and choosing, and they were expected to eat it in silence. 'Please' and 'Thank you' were permitted, but nothing more. Father and Mother might talk if they wanted to; but usually they were content to concentrate upon their enjoyment of the meal. Father might shovel green peas into his mouth with his knife, Mother might drink her tea from her saucer, and some of the children might lick their plates when the food was devoured; but who could eat peas with a two-pronged fork, or wait for tea to cool after the heat and flurry of cooking, and licking the plates passed as a graceful compliment to Mother's good dinner. 'Thank God for my good dinner. Thank Father and Mother. Amen' was the grace used in one family, and it certainly had the merit of giving credit where credit was due.

The Spiritual Home of the Tea-Pot

Agnes, Lady Jekyll (1861–1937), sister-in-law of Gertrude Jekyll, wrote a cookery column for The Times *in the early 1920s; the columns were published in 1922 as* Kitchen Essays.

For the generation now passing away, tea was only clandestinely procurable by joining the children, and still it seems to have a special charm out of nursery mugs with hot toast buttered over the high fender as only Nurse knows how to do it, or shared on the school-room hearthrug surrounded by jam-eating clamorous youth, when it tastes so much better than on the gilt chairs accompanied by decorous drawing-room conversation.

During the war years, even the office yielded to the allurements of afternoon tea, and the humour of its preparation by flappers, and its enjoyment by their principals, provided the caricaturist and the letter-writer to the papers with much happy inspiration and spiteful suggestion. Hungry hunters and shooters, triumphant and bemired from the chase love to quench their thirst and spoil their dinners under the stuffed heads in the great hall, and golfers and fishermen to magnify their exploits amid the miscellaneous companionship of the hotel lounge.

All these confess the hour with great pleasure, but the true spiritual home of the tea-pot is surely in a softly-lighted room, between a deep armchair and a sofa cushioned with Asiatic charm, two cups only, and these of thinnest china, awaiting their fragrant infusion, whilst the clock points nearer to six than five, and a wood fire flickers sympathetically on the hearth.

✕ Subtle and Voluptuous

MFK Fisher (1908–1992) was undoubtedly the most arresting and remarkable food-writer of the twentieth century. In Serve It Forth *(1937), she describes the simple delight of crisped tangerine sections.*

It was [in Strasbourg] that I discovered how to eat little dried sections of tangerine. My pleasure in them is subtle and voluptuous and quite inexplicable. I can only write how they are prepared.

In the morning, in the soft sultry chamber, sit in the window peeling tangerines, three or four. Peel them gently; do not bruise them, as you watch soldiers pour past and past the corner and over the canal towards the watched Rhine. Separate each plump little pregnant crescent. If you find the Kiss, the secret section, save it for Al.

Listen to the chambermaid thumping up the pillows, and murmur encouragement to her thick Alsatian tales of *l'intérieur*. That is Paris, the interior, Paris or anywhere west of Strasbourg or maybe the Vosges. While she mutters of seduction and French bicyclists who ride more than wheels, tear delicately from the soft pile of sections each velvet string. You know those white pulpy strings that hold tangerines into their skins? Tear them off. Be careful.

Take yesterday's paper (when we were in Strasbourg *L'Ami du Peuple* was best, because when it got hot the ink stayed on it) and spread it on top of the radiator. The maid has gone, of course - it might be hard to ignore her belligerent Alsatian glare of astonishment.

After you have put the pieces of tangerine on the paper on the hot radiator, it is best to forget about them. Al comes home, you go to a long noon dinner in the brown dining-room, afterwards maybe you have a little nip of quetsch from the bottle on the armoire. Finally he goes. Of course you are sorry, but –

On the radiator the sections of tangerines have grown even plumper, hot and full. You carry them to the window, pull it open, and leave them for a few minutes on the packed snow of the sill. They are ready.

All afternoon you can sit, then, looking down on the corner. Afternoon papers are delivered to the kiosk. Children come home from school just as three lovely whores mince smartly into the pension's chic tearoom. A basketful of Dutch tulips stations itself by the tram-stop, ready to tempt tired clerks at six o'clock. Finally the soldiers stump back from the Rhine. It is dark.

The sections of tangerine are gone, and I cannot tell you why they are so magical. Perhaps it is that little shell, thin as one layer of enamel on a Chinese bowl, that crackles so tinily, so ultimately under your teeth. Or the rush of cold pulp just after it. Or the perfume. I cannot tell.

There must be someone, though, who understands what I mean. Probably everyone does, because of his own secret eatings.

8 Literary Recipes

*One cannot think well, love well, sleep well,
if one has not dined well.*

Virginia Woolf

*It is a mistake to think you can solve any
major problems just with potatoes.*

Douglas Adams

CHOU DE MILAN DES VERTUS

Classical Cabbages

The Victorian horticulturist George Ellwanger (1816–1906) found these ideas for cooking greens in the collection of ancient Roman recipes now known as Apicius, *after the Roman gourmet Marcus Gavius Apicius, who was once thought to have compiled them.*

Broccoli was an especial favourite with Apicius, the most tender parts being boiled, with the addition of pepper, chopped onions, cumin and coriander seed bruised together, and a little oil and sun-made wine …
Asparagus, which Charles Lamb says inspires gentle thoughts, was culti-vated with notable care. The finest heads were dried, and when wanted were placed in hot water and boiled. Lucullus and Apicius ate only those that were grown in the environs of Nesis, a city of Campania.

Beets, mallows, artichokes, and cucumbers were greatly relished and elaborately prepared, and garlic, extolled by Virgil and decried by Horace, was generously used. Apicius, in his treatise De Re Culinaria, gives numerous recipes for cooking the cabbage – silken-leaved, curled, and hard white varieties:

1 Take only the most delicate and tender part of the cabbage, which boil, and then pour off the water; season it with cumin seed, salt, old wine, oil, pepper, Alexander [a celery-like plant], mint, rue, cori-ander seed, gravy, and oil.
2 Prepare the cabbage in the manner just mentioned, and make a seasoning of coriander seed, onion, cumin seed, pepper, a small quantity of oil, and wine made of sun raisins.
3 When you have boiled the cabbages in water put them into a saucepan and stew them with gravy, oil, wine, cumin seed, pepper, leeks, and green coriander.
4 Add to the preceding ingredients flour of almonds, and raisins dried in the sun.
5 Prepare them again in the above manner, and cook them with green olives.

✗ Unctuous Parsnips

Founder member of the Royal Society, friend of both Fermat and Ben Jonson, and an endless experimenter, Sir Kenelm Digby (1603–1665) invented this sumptuous recipe for parsnips stewed with milk.

Scrape well three or four good large roots, cleansing well their outside, and cutting off as much of the little end as is Fibrous, and of the great end as is hard. Put them into a possnet or pot, with about a quart of Milk upon them, or as much as will cover them in boiling, which do moderately, till you find they are very tender. This may be in an hour and half, sooner or later, as the roots are of a good kind. Then take them out, and scrape all the outside into a pulp, like the pulp of roasted apples, which put in a dish upon a chafing dish of Coals, with a little of the Milk, you boiled them in, put to them; not so much as to drown them, but only to imbibe them: and then with stewing, the pulp will imbibe all that Milk. When you see it is drunk in, put to the pulp a little more of the same Milk, and stew that, till it be drunk in. Continue doing thus till it hath drunk in a good quantity of the Milk, and is well swelled with it, and will take in no more, which may be in a good half hour. Eat them so, without Sugar or Butter; for they will have a natural sweetness that is beyond sugar, and will be Unctuous, so as not to need Butter.

✕ The Diarist as Cook

John Evelyn (1620–1706) filled volumes with notes on food and gardens, as well as all aspects of cultural and political life. The three recipes below (which I have slightly edited) would make a perfect dessert course. Evelyn made the wine for Sir Christopher Wren, who gave him the recipe.

TO STEW PIPPINS

Part and core a dozen pippins very neatly; cut them in halves as quick as you can put to them a pound of double-refined sugar, a pint of water, a few cloves, a little cinnamon, and a little fresh lemon peel; let them boil pretty quick. When the underside is clear, turn them; if the syrup grows thick put in 6 spoonfuls of water. When they are clear all over, lay them in a dish one by one, squeeze on some juice of lemon; strain the syrup over the apples and stick some citron and bits of preserved orange on every piece.

FROATH, OR WHIPT CREAM

Take a pint of white wine, and put to it the juice of two lemons, make it very sweet of the finest sugar, then put to it a quart of Cream, stirring it in, then immediately you must take a whisk made of dry birch twigs, and beat it as you do eggs, and as the froth riseth take it off with a spoon, and lay it like suds in a silver dish or the like. You must tie a bunch of Rosemary, and one of the Lemon peels in the whisk, before you beat it.

GOOSEBERRY WINE

Take gooseberries dropping ripe next to rottenness, squeeze them to a mash thick as mustard, let it work and be well skimmed, tun up the clear and it will ferment again; being kept 2 years it is an excellent wine.

✕ How to Dress a Trout and a Grayling

Izaak Walton (1594–1683) made Piscator and Viator, the fishermen in his Compleat Angler *(1653), as interested in how to cook fish as in how to catch them.*

Pisc. Now, sir, what think you of our river Dove?

Viat. I think it to be the best trout-river in England; and am so far in love with it, that if it were mine, and that I could keep it to myself, I would not exchange that water for all the land it runs over, to be totally debarred from it.

Pisc. That compliment to the river, speaks you a true lover of the art of angling: and now, sir, to make part of amends for sending you so uncivilly out alone this morning, I will myself dress you this dish of fish for your dinner; walk but into the parlour, you will find one book or other in the window to entertain you the while; and you shall have it presently.

Viat. Well, sir, I obey you.

Pisc. Look you, sir! have I not made haste?

Viat. Believe me, sir, that you have; and it looks so well, I long to be at it.

Pisc. Fall to then. Now, sir, what say you, am I a tolerable cook or no?

Viat. So good a one, that I did never eat so good fish in my life. This fish is infinitely better than any I ever tasted of the kind in my life. 'Tis quite another thing than our trouts about London.

Pisc. You would say so, if that trout you eat of were in right season: but pray eat of the grayling, which, upon my word, at this time, is by much the better fish.

Viat. In earnest, and so it is. And I have one request to make to you, which is, that as you have taught me to catch trout and grayling, you will now teach me how to dress them as these are dressed; which, questionless, is of all other the best way.

Pisc. That I will, sir, with all my heart; and am glad you like them so well, as to make that request. And they are dressed thus:

1—1 Red Mullet. 2 Grayling. 3 John Dory. 4 Mackerel. 5 Cod. 6 Whiting. 7 Salmon.
8 Herring. 9 Plaice. 10 Flounder. 11 Gurnet. 12 Crayfish.

Take your trout, wash, and dry him with a clean napkin; then open him, and having taken out his guts, and all the blood, wipe him very clean within, but wash him not; and give him three scotches with a knife to the bone, on one side only. After which take a clean kettle, and put in as much hard stale beer (but it must not be dead), vinegar, and a little white wine, and water, as will cover the fish you intend to boil: then throw into the liquor a good quantity of salt, the rind of a lemon, a handful of sliced horse-radish-root, with a handsome little faggot of rosemary, thyme, and winter-savory. Then set your kettle upon a quick fire of wood, and let your liquor boil up to the height before you put in your fish: and then, if there be many, put them in one by one, that they may not so cool the liquor, as to make it fall. And whilst your fish is boiling, beat up the butter for your sauce with a ladle-full or two of the liquor it is boiling in, and, being boiled enough, immediately pour the liquor from the fish: and, being laid in a dish, pour your butter upon it; and, stewing it plentifully over with shaved horse-radish, and a little pounded ginger; garnish your sides for your dish, and the fish itself with a sliced lemon or two, and serve it up.

A grayling is also to be dressed exactly after the same manner, saving that he is to be scaled, which a trout never is; and that must be done, either with one's nails, or very lightly and carefully with a knife for bruising the fish. And note that these kinds of fish, a trout especially, if he is not eaten within four or five hours after he is taken, is worth nothing.

✗ Oh, the Charming White and Red

In this poem, Jonathan Swift (1667–1745) offers excellent details as to the best way of cooking and serving mutton. I can recommend the appetiser of dripping-soaked toast.

Gently stir and blow the fire,
Lay the mutton down to roast,
Dress it quickly, I desire,
In the dripping put a toast,
That I hunger may remove
Mutton is the meat I love.

On the dresser see it lie;
Oh, the charming white and red;
Finer meat ne'er met the eye,
On the sweetest grass it fed:
Let the jack go swiftly round,
Let me have it nice and brown'd.
On the table spread the cloth,
Let the knives be sharp and clean,
Pickles get and salad both,
Let them each be fresh and green.
With small beer, good ale and wine,
Oh ye gods! how I shall dine.

✖ Elegiac Mutton Sauces

Thomas Gray (1716–1771) wrote down these recipes on a blank page in his own copy of William Verrall's Complete System of Cookery *(1759).*

When the shoulder of mutton is three parts roasted, put under it a plate with a little water, 2 to 3 spoonfuls of Claret, some sliced onion or shallot, a little grated nutmeg, one anchovy washed and minced, a little bit of butter. Let the meat drip into it, and when it is enough, run the sauce through a sieve, and stir in a little cider-vinegar.

OR

Take the same ingredients, with the juice of an orange: stew them together a little, and pour to the gravy, that runs from the meat.

✕ An Omelette for Madame de Récamier

With no apparent logic, Isabella Beeton (1836–1865) positioned this delightful anecdote and recipe at the end of a chapter devoted to sweets and syllabubs in the 1861 edition of her Book of Household Management.

'Every one knows,' says Brillat-Savarin, in his *Physiology of Taste*, 'that for twenty years Madame Récamier was the most beautiful woman in Paris. It is also well known that she was exceedingly charitable, and took a great interest in every benevolent work. Wishing to consult the Curé of – respecting the working of an institution, she went to his house at five o'clock in the afternoon, and was much astonished at finding him already at his dinner-table.

'Madame Récamier wished to retire, but the Curé would not hear of it. A neat white cloth covered the table; some good old wine sparkled in a crystal decanter; the porcelain was of the best; the plates had heaters of boiling water beneath them; a neatly-costumed maid-servant was in attendance. The repast was a compromise between frugality and luxury. The crawfish-soup had just been removed, and there was on the table a salmon-trout, an omelette, and a salad.

'"My dinner will tell you," said the worthy Curé, with a smile, "that it is fast-day, according to our Church's regulations." Madame Récamier and her host attacked the trout, the sauce served with which betrayed a skilful hand, the countenance of the Curé the while showing satisfaction.

'And now they fell upon the omelette, which was round, sufficiently thick, and cooked, so to speak, to a hair's-breadth.

'As the spoon entered the omelette, a thick rich juice issued from it, pleasant to the eye as well as to the smell; the dish became full of it; and our fair friend owns that, between the perfume and the sight, it made her mouth water.

'"It is an *omelette au thon* (that is to say, a tunny omelette)," said the Curé, noticing, with the greatest delight, the emotion of Madame Récamier, "and few people taste it without lavishing praises on it."

'"It surprises me not at all," returned the beauty; "never has so enticing an omelette met my gaze at any of our lay tables."

"'My cook understands them well, I think.'"

"'Yes,' added Madame, 'I never ate anything so delightful.'"

'Then came a salad, which Savarin recommends to all who place confidence in him. It refreshes without exciting; and he has a theory that it makes people younger.

'Amidst pleasant converse the dessert arrived. It consisted of three apples, cheese, and a plate of preserves; and then upon a little round table was served the Mocha coffee, for which France has been, and is, so justly famous.

"'I never,' said the Curé, "take spirits; I always offer liqueurs to my guests but reserve the use of them myself to my old age, if it should please Providence to grant me that."

'Finally, the charming Madame Récamier took her leave, and told all her friends of the delicious omelette which she had seen and partaken of.'

And Brillat Savarin, in his capacity as the Layard of the concealed treasures of Gastronomia, has succeeded in withdrawing from obscurity the details of the preparation of which so much had been said, and which he imagines to be as wholesome as it was agreeable. Here follows the recipe:-

OMELETTE AU THON

Take, for 6 persons, the roes of 2 carp; (note: An American writer says he has followed this recipe, substituting pike, shad, &c., in the place of carp, and can recommend all these also, with a quiet conscience. Any fish, indeed, may be used with success).

Bleach them, by putting them, for 5 minutes, in boiling water slightly salted. Take a piece of fresh tunny about the size of a hen's egg, to which add a small shallot already chopped; hash up together the roe and the tunny, so as to mix them well, and throw the whole into a saucepan, with a sufficient quantity of very good butter: whip it up until the butter is melted! This constitutes the specialty of the omelette. Take a second piece of butter − à discrétion, mix it with parsley and herbs, place it in a long-shaped dish destined to receive the omelette; squeeze the juice of a lemon over it, and place it on hot embers. Beat up 12 eggs (the fresher the better); throw up the sauté of roe and tunny, stirring it so as to mix all well together; then make your omelette in the usual manner, endeavouring to turn it out long, thick, and soft. Spread it carefully on the dish prepared for it, and serve at once. This dish ought to be reserved for recherché déjeûners, or for assemblies where amateurs meet who know how to eat well; washed down with a good old wine, it will work wonders.

Note: The roe and the tunny must be beaten up (sauté) without allowing them to boil, to prevent their hardening, which would prevent them mixing well with the eggs. Your dish should be hollowed towards the centre, to allow the gravy to concentrate, that it may be helped with a spoon. The dish ought to be slightly heated, otherwise the cold china will extract all the heat from the omelette.

Creme à la
Jenny Lind

...leman
...as been
...rom acute
...e body and
...utterly
...to attend to
...fficial
...s" for the
...weeks —

✕ Soup for the Swedish Nightingale

'Mademoiselle Lind was in the habit of taking this soup before she sang, as she found the sago and eggs soothing to the chest, and beneficial to the voice,' explains Eliza Acton in a note on this very substantial broth, which she included in her Modern Cookery for Private Families Reduced to a System of Easy Practice. *First published in 1845,* Modern Cookery *became a bestseller, setting the tone for future cookery books by listing ingredients and giving cooking times.*

MADEMOISELLE JENNY LIND'S SOUP (AUTHENTIC RECEIPT)
This receipt does not merely bear the name of 'Mademoiselle Lind', but is in reality that of the soup which was constantly served to her, as it was prepared by her own cook. We are indebted for it to the kindness of the very popular Swedish authoress, Miss Bremer, who received it direct from her accomplished countrywoman.
The following proportions are for a tureen of this excellent potage:

Wash a quarter of a pound of the best pearl sago until the water poured from it is clear; then stew it quite tender and very thick in water or thick broth (it will require nearly or quite a quart of liquid, which should be poured to it cold, and heated slowly): then mix gradually with it a pint of good boiling cream, and the yolks of four fresh eggs, and mingle the whole carefully with two quarts of strong veal or beef stock, which should always be kept ready boiling. Send the soup immediately to table.

✗ Herring à la Rob Roy

Alexis Soyer (1810–1858) offered this tribute to Sir Walter Scott in the final chapter of Culinary Campaign *(1857), his spirited autobiographical account of the (immense) contribution he made to the Crimean War effort by joining the troops at his own expense and organising camp kitchens in Scutari. It was billed as a suitable addition to the menus offered by such London eateries as Simpson's in the Strand.*

Well wash and clean a red herring, wipe it dry and place it in a pie dish, having cut off the head, and split it in two up the back, put a gill or two of whisky over the herring, according to size, hold it on one side of the dish, so that it is covered with the spirit, set it alight, and when the flame goes out the fish is done.

✗ Balaklava Nectar

The last recipe in Soyer's collection was a celebratory tipple.

Thinly peel the rind of half a lemon, shred it fine, and put it into a punch bowl; add 2 tablespoons of crushed sugar and the juice of two lemons, the half of a small cucumber sliced with the peel on; toss it up several times; then add two bottles of soda-water, 2 of claret, 1 of champagne, stir well together and serve.

✕ A Load of Bosh

'Our readers will be interested in the following communications from our valued and learned contributor, Professor Bosh, whose labours in the fields of Culinary and Botanical science, are so well known to all the world,' wrote Edward Lear (1812–1888) in what he claimed was the August 1870 issue of the (non-existent) Nonsense Gazette. *'The first three articles richly merit to be added to the domestic cookery of every family'* (Nonsense Songs, Stories, Botany and Alphabets, *1871).*

AMBLONGUS PIE

Take 4 pounds (say 4½ pounds) of fresh Amblongusses, and put them in a small pipkin.

Cover them with water and boil them for 8 hours incessantly, after which add 2 pints of new milk, and proceed to boil for 4 hours more.

When you have ascertained that the Amblongusses are quite soft, take them out and place them in a wide pan, taking care to shake them well previously.

Grate some nutmeg over the surface, and cover them carefully with powdered gingerbread, curry-powder, and a sufficient quantity of Cayenne pepper.

Remove the pan into the next room, and place it on the floor. Bring it back again, and let it simmer for three-quarters of an hour. Shake the pan violently till all the Amblongusses have become a pale purple colour.

Then, having prepared a paste, insert the whole carefully, adding at the same time a small pigeon, 2 slices of beef, 4 cauliflowers, and any number of oysters.

Watch patiently till the crust begins to rise, and add a pinch of salt from time to time.

Serve up in a clean dish, and throw the whole out of the window as fast as possible.

CRUMBOBBLIOUS CUTLETS

Procure some strips of beef, and having cut them into the smallest possible slices, proceed to cut them still smaller, eight or perhaps nine times.

When the whole is thus minced, brush it up hastily with a new clothes-brush, and stir round rapidly and capriciously with a salt-spoon or a soup ladle.

Place the whole in a saucepan, and remove it to a sunny place, – say the roof of the house if free from sparrows or other birds, – and leave it there for about a week.

At the end of that time add a little lavender, some oil of almonds, and a few herring-bones; and cover the whole with 4 gallons of clarified crumbobblious sauce, when it will be ready for use.

Cut it into the shape of ordinary cutlets, and serve it up in a clean tablecloth or dinner-napkin.

GOSKY PATTIES

Take a pig, three or four years of age, and tie him by the off-hind leg to a post. Place 5 pounds of currants, 3 of sugar, 2 pecks of peas, 18 roast chestnuts, a candle, and six bushels of turnips, within his reach; if he eats these, constantly provide him with more.

Then procure some cream, some slices of Cheshire cheese, four quires of foolscap paper, and a packet of black pins. Work the whole into a paste, and spread it out to dry on a sheet of clean brown water-proof linen.

When the paste is perfectly dry, but not before, proceed to beat the Pig violently, with the handle of a large broom. If he squeals, beat him again.

Visit the paste and beat the pig alternately for some days, and ascertain that if at the end of that period the whole is about to turn into Gosky Patties.

If it does not then, it never will; and in that case the Pig may be let loose, and the whole process may be considered as finished.

✗ Alexandre Dumas' Arab Omelette

As well as novels, Alexandre Dumas (1802–1870) wrote the sadly unfinished Grand dictionnaire de cuisine. *Posthumously published in 1873, it sparkles with wit as well as good sense. As a young man, he had travelled widely, publishing* Impressions of Travel, in Egypt and Arabia Petræa *in 1839. I love his confidence that exotic eggs were easily available from local zoos: modern cooks can substitute those of hens, ducks or geese.*

Ostrich and flamingo eggs, full and fresh, are now to be found almost everywhere, thanks to the zoological societies which have been founded even in towns of secondary importance. Thus an ostrich egg is today sold for one franc, and is equal in content to about ten hen's eggs.

This is how to make an Arab omelette.

Chop a fresh onion, put it in a frying pan with half a glass of olive oil, let it soften without colouring, and add the flesh of two large sweet peppers, after having grilled them for a few moments in order to remove the skin.

Add two good peeled and seeded tomatoes, cut in small pieces. Season this first preparation with a little salt and a touch of cayenne. Reduce some of the liquid given off by the tomatoes, then take the frying pan off the fire and add to its contents four anchovy fillets.

Now, as a separate operation, rub the bottom of a terrine with a clove of garlic. Pierce an ostrich or flamingo egg at both ends, so that you can blow out the whole and the yolk, causing them to fall into the terrine. Season, and beat with a fork.

Finally, pour a quarter of a glass of olive oil into an omelette pan. When it is thoroughly hot, pour in the eggs, let the omelette set, and add to it the mixture which you prepared earlier. Turn it over, keeping it flat, sprinkle a little more oil over it, and two seconds later slide it on to a round platter.

✕ Gelée Crème de Menthe

Agnes Jekyll (1861–1937) described this in her Kitchen Essays *(1922) as 'an emerald-green pool, set in a flat glass bowl, reminiscent of Sabrina fair in her home below translucent waves, or of Capri caverns, cool and deep'.*

Make a quart of good lemon jelly in the approved way, preferably with calves' feet, more probably with the best leaf gelatine, but not – oh! not – with jelly powders. Whilst warm, add a handful of those large green peppermint geranium leaves, thick as a fairy's blanket, soft as a vicuna robe, and to be found in most old-fashioned gardens, and let them flavour your blend; or you can use 3 or 4 drops of essence of peppermint, ½ teaspoonful of apple green to colour, or homemade spinach greening for a substitute. Pass through your jelly bag and serve very cold. A glass of crème de menthe might well improve this, but is by no means indispensable.

✗ Emily Dickinson's Gingerbread

Emily Dickinson (1830–1886) enjoyed cooking enormously, especially bread and puddings. 'I am going to learn to make bread tomorrow,' runs her letter to Abiah Root, her schoolmate and lifelong friend. 'So you may imagine me with my sleeves rolled up, mixing flour, milk, salaratus, etc, with a great deal of grace. I advise you if you don't know how to make the staff of life to learn with dispatch.' (Letters, September 25, 1845.) This recipe for gingerbread in Emily's handwriting survives among her manuscripts. It appears on the excellent Paper&Salt blog (paperandsalt.org).

1 quart [four cups] flour
½ cup butter
½ cup cream
1 tablespoon ginger
1 teaspoon soda
1 teaspoon salt
Molasses (about one cup)

Cream the butter and mix with lightly whipped cream. Sift dry ingredients together and combine with other ingredients. Make up with molasses. The dough is stiff and needs to be pressed into whatever pan you choose. A round or small square pan is suitable. The recipe also fits perfectly into a cast iron muffin pan, if you happen to have one which makes oval cakes. Bake at 350 F for 20 to 25 minutes.

✗ Omelette Arnold Bennett

I discovered this recipe from the kitchens of London's Savoy Hotel in my own favourite cookbook, Theodora FitzGibbon's The Art of British Cookery *(1965). Arnold Bennett regularly ordered it for a post-theatre meal. It has been elaborated upon countless times since, but is best kept simple.*

1 cup smoked haddock, filleted
6 eggs
2 tablespoons of cream
1 teaspoon of butter
2 tablespoons Parmesan cheese, grated
salt and pepper

Flake the lightly-cooked fish and mix with the grated Parmesan. Season to taste, and keep warm. Beat the eggs and melt the butter in a frying pan.

Keep the pan hot, but do not let the butter brown. Pour in the eggs and stir them once or twice, tipping the pan so that the eggs run all over it. Put the fish and cheese mixture on top and let the omelette get golden brown underneath. Pour over the cream and finish for 2 minutes under a hot grill.

Do not attempt to fold this omelette: it is made in the Spanish style, and is slid, cream side up, on to a hot plate.

✗ Orange Soufflé

Katherine Mansfield (1888–1923) loved eating and writing about eating.
'Curse them,' she said of the Swiss. 'The FOOD. It's got no nerves. You know
what I mean? It seems to lie down and wait for you; the very steaks are meek
… As to the purée de pommes de terre, you feel inclined to call it "uncle".' She
jotted down many recipes, including this one for orange soufflé, which survives
in her own handwriting; I also found this on the Paper&Salt blog.

Grate the rind of one orange, & one lemon, put into saucepan with
the juice of each, the yolks of three eggs & half a breakfast cup of sugar,
stir this until it becomes the thickness of honey, beat up the whites of
eggs to a <u>stiff</u> froth, & add to juice base, <u>not</u> letting it boil furiously, just
for a few minutes to become well mixed then turn into dish with or
without sponge cake at bottom, sopped in sherry wine & raspberry
jam; under these final conditions it would be called a <u>party</u> pudding!

✕ An After-Love Drink

Reputedly aphrodisiac ingredients such as nutmeg, cinnamon, truffles, anchovies and egg yolks recur frequently in Norman Douglas' (1868–1952) famous hymn to Aphrodite, Venus in the Kitchen. *Presumably his elderly friends were hoping for a second bite at the cherry after this post-coital pick-me-up.*

Into a Madeira glass pour: a quarter glass of maraschino, a yolk of egg, a quarter glass of cream, a quarter glass of old brandy. Serve without mixing, seeing that the yolk of the egg is not broken. The whole should be swallowed in one gulp.

Highly recommended by my friend Baron de M …

✗ A Nice Cup of Tea

George Orwell (1903–1950) gave his preferred method of brewing tea in an Evening Standard *article published on 12 January, 1946.*

If you look up 'tea' in the first cookery book that comes to hand you will probably find that it is unmentioned; or at most you will find a few lines of sketchy instructions which give no ruling on several of the most important points.

This is curious, not only because tea is one of the main stays of civilization in this country, as well as in Eire, Australia and New Zealand, but because the best manner of making it is the subject of violent disputes.

When I look through my own recipe for the perfect cup of tea, I find no fewer than eleven outstanding points. On perhaps two of them there would be pretty general agreement, but at least four others are acutely controversial. Here are my own eleven rules, every one of which I regard as golden:

First of all, one should use Indian or Ceylonese tea. China tea has virtues which are not to be despised nowadays – it is economical, and one can drink it without milk – but there is not much stimulation in it. One does not feel wiser, braver or more optimistic after drinking it. Anyone who has used that comforting phrase 'a nice cup of tea' invariably means Indian tea.

Secondly, tea should be made in small quantities – that is, in a teapot. Tea out of an urn is always tasteless, while army tea, made in a cauldron, tastes of grease and whitewash. The teapot should be made of china or earthenware. Silver or Britanniaware teapots produce inferior tea and enamel pots are worse; though curiously enough a pewter teapot (a rarity nowadays) is not so bad.

Thirdly, the pot should be warmed beforehand. This is better done by placing it on the hob than by the usual method of swilling it out with hot water.

Fourthly, the tea should be strong. For a pot holding a quart, if you are going to fill it nearly to the brim, six heaped teaspoons would be about right. In a time of rationing, this is not an idea that can be

realized on every day of the week, but I maintain that one strong cup of tea is better than twenty weak ones. All true tea lovers not only like their tea strong, but like it a little stronger with each year that passes – a fact which is recognized in the extra ration issued to old-age pensioners.

Fifthly, the tea should be put straight into the pot. No strainers, muslin bags or other devices to imprison the tea. In some countries teapots are fitted with little dangling baskets under the spout to catch the stray leaves, which are supposed to be harmful. Actually one can swallow tea-leaves in considerable quantities without ill effect, and if the tea is not loose in the pot it never infuses properly.

Sixthly, one should take the teapot to the kettle and not the other way about. The water should be actually boiling at the moment of impact, which means that one should keep it on the flame while one pours. Some people add that one should only use water that has been freshly brought to the boil, but I have never noticed that it makes any difference.

Seventhly, after making the tea, one should stir it, or better, give the pot a good shake, afterwards allowing the leaves to settle.

Eighthly, one should drink out of a good breakfast cup – that is, the cylindrical type of cup, not the flat, shallow type. The breakfast cup holds more, and with the other kind one's tea is always half cold before one has well started on it.

Ninthly, one should pour the cream off the milk before using it for tea. Milk that is too creamy always gives tea a sickly taste.

Tenthly, one should pour tea into the cup first. This is one of the most controversial points of all; indeed in every family in Britain there are probably two schools of thought on the subject. The milk-first school can bring forward some fairly strong arguments, but I maintain that my own argument is unanswerable. This is that, by putting the tea in first and stirring as one pours, one can exactly regulate the amount of milk whereas one is liable to put in too much milk if one does it the other way round.

Lastly, tea – unless one is drinking it in the Russian style – should be drunk without sugar. I know very well that I am in a minority here. But still, how can you call yourself a true tea-lover if you destroy the flavour of your tea by putting sugar in it? It would be equally reasonable to put in pepper or salt. Tea is meant to be bitter, just as beer is meant to be bitter. If you sweeten it, you are no longer tasting the tea, you are merely tasting the sugar; you could make a very similar drink by dissolving sugar in plain hot water.

Some people would answer that they don't like tea in itself, that they only drink it in order to be warmed and stimulated, and they need sugar to take the taste away. To those misguided people I would say: Try drinking tea without sugar for, say, a fortnight and it is very unlikely that you will ever want to ruin your tea by sweetening it again.

These are not the only controversial points to arise in connexion with tea drinking, but they are sufficient to show how subtilized the whole business has become. There is also the mysterious social etiquette surrounding the teapot (why is it considered vulgar to drink out of your saucer, for instance?) and much might be written about the subsidiary uses of tea leaves, such as telling fortunes, predicting the arrival of visitors, feeding rabbits, healing burns and sweeping the carpet. It is worth paying attention to such details as warming the pot and using water that is really boiling, so as to make quite sure of wringing out of one's ration the twenty good, strong cups that two ounces, properly handled, ought to represent.

✗ Cauliflowers in Dijon

MFK Fisher published her The Gastronomical Me *in 1943; it celebrated her discovery of the delights of French cooking when she came from America to live in Dijon as a young bride.*

There in Dijon, the cauliflowers were very small and succulent, grown in that ancient soil. I separated the flowerets and dropped them in boiling water for just a few minutes. Then I drained them and put them in a wide shallow casserole, and covered them with heavy cream, and a thick sprinkling of freshly grated Gruyère, the nice rubbery kind that didn't come from Switzerland at all, but from the Jura. It was called 'râpé' in the market, and was grated while you watched, in a soft cloudy pile, onto your piece of paper.

I put some fresh pepper over the top, and in a way I can't remember now the little tin oven heated the whole thing and melted the cheese and browned it. As soon as that happened we ate it.

The cream and cheese had come together into a perfect sauce, and the little flowers were tender and fresh. We cleaned our plates with bits of crisp bread crust and drank the wine, and Al and Lawrence planned to write books about Aristotle and Robinson Jeffers and probably themselves, and I planned a few things, too.

✕ Clotted Cream

'Alas! You never see real Devonshire cream in Devon nowadays – not as it used to be – scalded and taken off the milk in layers.' Miss Marple's appetite for clotted cream echoed that of her creator Agatha Christie (1890–1976), who spooned it from a huge cup with 'Don't Be Greedy' on it as she worked at her typewriter. You need access to a milking cow to make the real thing, but fresh full-cream milk can be substituted.

Use new milk and strain at once, as soon as milked, into shallow pans. Allow it to stand for 24 hours in winter and 12 hours in summer. Then put the pan on the stove, or better still into a steamer containing water, and let it slowly heat until the cream begins to show a raised ring round the edge. When sufficiently cooked, place in a cool dairy and leave for 12 or 24 hours. Great care must be taken in moving the pans so that the cream is not broken, both in putting on the fire and taking off. When required skim off the cream in layers into a glass dish for the table, taking care to have a good 'crust' on the top. (Edith Martin, *Cornish Recipes Ancient & Modern*, Women's Institute, 1929)

✗ Avocados are My Favourite Fruit

The poet and novelist Sylvia Plath (1932–1963) loved food, and excelled in descriptions of it: 'Eight combs of yellow cups, And the hive itself a teacup' (honey), the 'scraggly-lace, blue-eyed peacockish shells' (oysters). In her auto-biographical novel The Bell-Jar *(1963), she describes her preferred way of eating avocados.*

Avocados are my favourite fruit. Every Sunday my grandfather used to bring me an avocado pear hidden at the bottom of his briefcase under six soiled shirts and the Sunday comics. He taught me how to eat avocados by melting grape jelly and french dressing together in a saucepan and filling the cup of the pear with the garnet sauce. I felt homesick for that sauce.

✂ Scripture Cake

This traditional recipe requires its makers to have more than a nodding acquaint-ance with the Bible, and is said to have been used as a scriptural teaching tool for centuries. Cheats can use the key below.

INGREDIENTS
¾ cup Genesis 18:8
1½ cups Jeremiah 6:20
5 Isaiah 10:14 (separated)
3 cups sifted Leviticus 24:5
3 teaspoons 2 Kings 2:20
3 teaspoons Amos 4:5
1 teaspoon Exodus 30:23
1 teaspoon 2 Chronicles 9:9
½ cup Judges 4:19
¾ cup chopped Genesis 43:11
¾ cup finely cut Jeremiah 24:5
¾ cup 2 Samuel 16:1
¾ cup Genesis 24:45

Cream Genesis 18 with Jeremiah 6. Beat in yolks of Isaiah 10, one at a time. Sift together Leviticus 24; 2 Kings 2; Amos 4; Exodus 30; and 2 Chronicles 9.

Blend into creamed mixture alternately with Judges 4. Beat whites of Isaiah 10 till stiff; fold in. Fold in chopped Genesis 43; Jeremiah 24; and 2 Samuel 16. Turn into a 10-inch pan that has been greased and dusted with Leviticus 24.

Bake for and hour and ten minutes at 325 degrees F until it is golden brown or Gabriel blows his trumpet, whichever happens first. Remove from oven. After fifteen minutes, remove it from the pan. Cool completely. Drizzle over it some Burnt Jeremiah Syrup.

Burnt Jeremiah Syrup
INGREDIENTS
1½ cups Jeremiah 6:20
½ cup Genesis 24:45
¼ cup Genesis 18:8

Melt Jeremiah 6 in a heavy skillet over low heat. Keep cooking it till it is a deep gold, then add Genesis 24. Cook till smooth and remove from the heat. Add Genesis 18 and stir till it melts, then cool.

After drizzling this on the Scripture Cake, you can decorate it with flaked Genesis 43.

KEY TO THE SCRIPTURE CAKE: INGREDIENTS ARE IN BOLD
Genesis 18:8 'And he took **butter**, and milk, and the calf which he had dressed, and set it before them.'

Jeremiah 6:20 'To what purpose cometh there to me frankincense from Sheba, and the sweet cane [**sugar**] from a far country.'

Isaiah 10:14 'And my hand hath found as a nest the riches of the peoples; and as one gathered **eggs** that are forsaken, have I gathered the earth.'

Leviticus 24:5 'And thou shalt take **fine flour**, and bake twelve cakes thereof.'

2 Kings 2:20 'And he said, Bring me a new cruse, and put **salt** therein.'

Amos 4:5 'And offer a sacrifice of thanksgiving of that which is leavened [**baking powder**], and proclaim free will offerings and publish them.'

Exodus 30:23 'Take thou also, unto thee the chief spices; of flowering myrrh five hundred shekels, and of **sweet cinnamon** half as much.'

2 Chronicles 9:9 'And she gave the King a hundred and twenty talents of gold, and spices in great abundance [**mixed spice**].'

Judges 4:19 'And he said unto her, Give me, I pray thee, a little water to drink; for I am thirsty. And she opened a bottle of **milk** and gave him drink.'

Genesis 43:11 'Carry down the man a present, a little balm, and a little honey, spicery and myrrh, nuts and **almonds**.'

Jeremiah 24:5 'Thou saith Jehovah, God of Israel: Like these good **figs**, so will I regard the captives of Judah whom I have sent out of this place into the land of the Chaldeans, for good.'

2 Samuel 16:1 'And when David was a little past the top of the assent, behold, Ziba, the servant of Mephiboseth met him, with a couple of asses saddled, and upon them two hundred loaves of bread, and a hundred clusters of **raisins**.'

Genesis 24:45 'And before I had done speaking in my heart, behold Rebekah came forth with her pitcher [**water**] on her shoulder; and she went down to the fountain, and drew: and I said unto her, Let me drink, I pray thee.'

And for the seriously lazy, here are the key words from the Bible in order of appearance in the recipe: butter, sugar, eggs, fine flour, salt, leavened [baking powder], sweet cinnamon, spices [mixed spice], milk, almonds, figs, raisins, water.

LIST OF ILLUSTRATIONS

All images are from the collections of the British Library unless otherwise stated.

housewife or ménagère. Comprising nearly one thousand receipts ... Second edition by Alexis Soyer, 1849 (1608/5543).

p. 146 An Australian Kitchen, from The book of household management ... Entirely new edition, revised and corrected, with new coloured engravings by Isabella Beeton, 1892 (7942.dd.9).

p. 148 Preparing sweetmeats for Sultan Ghiyath al-Din, miniature from The Ni'matnama-i Nasir al-Din Shah [A manuscript on Indian cookery and the preparation of sweetmeats, spices etc.], c. 1495– 1505 (I.O. Islamic 149, f.118v).

p. 150 A Greek Banquet, illustration by G. Scharf from Manners and Customs of the Greeks by Theodor Panofka, 1849 (7707.e.31).

p. 154 Banquet at a wealthy home in ancient Rome, hand-coloured nineteenth-century woodcut. Akg-images/North Wind Picture Archives.

p. 160 Preparing sweetmeats for Sultan Ghiyath al-Din, miniature from The Ni'matnama-i Nasir al-Din Shah [A manuscript on Indian cookery and the preparation of sweetmeats, spices etc.], c. 1495– 1505 (I.O. Islamic 149, f.83v).

p. 169 An American Stove, illustration from The book of household management ... Entirely new edition, revised and corrected, with new coloured engravings by Isabella Beeton, 1892 (7942.dd.9).

p. 172 Dinner and Dessert China, illustration from The book of household management ... Entirely new edition, revised and corrected, with new coloured engravings by Isabella Beeton, 1892 (7942.dd.9).

p. 175 'Though ye have lain among the pots yet shall ye be as the wings of a dove', illustration by Jessie Wilcox Smith from Scribners Magazine, 1903 (P.P.6383.ac).

p. 179 K for Kitchen Stuff, illustration to George Cruikshank's 'Comic Alphabet' , 1836. British Museum.

p. 184 Woodcut by Eric Ravilious from The Country Life cookery book: with a few hints and reminders about the kitchen garden by Ambrose Heath, 1937 (7941.ppp.45).

p. 187 Illustration by Ian Ribbons from Three Men in a Boat, to say nothing of the dog! by Jerome K. Jerome, 1964 (Cup.502.c.22). © Ian Ribbons.

p. 191 The Modern Mode of Serving Dishes: Scalloped Oysters and Dressed Lobster, illustration from The Book of Household Management, etc. by Isabella Beeton, 1861 (C.194.a.507).

p. 192 'Reflects at his club...', illustration by Randolph Caldecott from The complete collection of Randolph Caldecott's contributions to the 'Graphic' (VXf3/2616).

p. 196 Illustration by Dudley Hardy from Homes of the Passing Show. Sketches written by Beatty Kingston, R. Hichens, ... and others, 1900 (10350.dd.7).

p. 200 Illustration by Carl Larsson from Jugend, 1905 (P.P.4736.hea).

p. 202 Cabbage , illustration from Album Vilmorin, by Pierre Philippe André Lévêque de Vilmorin, 1850 (N.Tab.2004/11).

p. 207 Fish, illustration from The Book of Household Management, etc. by Isabella Beeton, 1861 (C.194.a.507).

p. 210 The position of the hands when mixing, illustration from The royal cookery book (Le livre de cuisine) by Jules Gouffé, 1883 (RB.23.b.6278).

p. 215 'Symposium Gastronomicum of all Nations. The Renowned Soyer exhibiting his Magic Stove', from The House that Paxton built by G. A. Sala, 1851 (012331.de.83).

p. 220 Vanilla Cream, illustration from The royal cookery book (Le livre de cuisine) by Jules Gouffé, 1883 (RB.23.b.6278).

p. 222 The Chef at the Savoy, illustration by Dudley Hardy from Homes of the Passing Show. Sketches written by Beatty Kingston, R. Hichens, ... and others, 1900 (10350.dd.7).

p. 224 Tangerine Soufflé, illustration from The Ideal Cookery Book by Margarte Alice Fairclough, 1914 (7850.g.12).

p. 227 Breakfast and tea china, illustration from The book of household management ... Entirely new edition, revised and corrected, with new coloured engravings by Isabella Beeton, 1892 (7942.dd.9).

INDEX OF AUTHORS

First published in 2015 by
The British Library
96 Euston Road
London NW1 2DB

Cataloguing in Publication Data
A catalogue record for this publication is available from
The British Library

ISBN 978 0 7123 5780 7

Designed and typeset by Briony Hartley, Goldust Design
Picture research by Sally Nicholls
Printed in Malta by Gutenberg Press